CultureShock!
A Survival Guide to Customs and Etiquette

Scotland

Jamie Grant

Marshall Cavendish
Editions

This 4th edition published in 2009 by:
Marshall Cavendish Corporation
99 White Plains Road
Tarrytown NY 10591-9001
www.marshallcavendish.us

First published in 2001 by Times Media Pte Ltd; 2nd edition published in 2003;
3rd edition published in 2006.
© 2009 Marshall Cavendish International (Asia) Private Limited
All rights reserved

Other Marshall Cavendish Offices:
Marshall Cavendish International (Asia) Pte Ltd. 1 New Industrial Road,
Singapore 536196 ■ Marshall Cavendish Ltd. 5th Floor, 32-38 Saffron Hill,
London EC1N 8FH, UK ■ Marshall Cavendish International (Thailand) Co Ltd.
253 Asoke, 12th Flr, Sukhumvit 21 Road, Klongtoey Nua, Wattana, Bangkok
10110, Thailand ■ Marshall Cavendish (Malaysia) Sdn Bhd, Times Subang,
Lot 46, Subang Hi-Tech Industrial Park, Batu Tiga, 40000 Shah Alam, Selangor
Darul Ehsan, Malaysia

Marshall Cavendish is a trademark of Times Publishing Limited

ISBN: 978-0-7614-5675-9

Please contact the publisher for the Library of Congress catalogue number

Printed in Singapore by Times Printers Pte Ltd

Photo Credits:
All black and white photos from the author except page 121 (Ceara Conway).
All colour images from Photolibrary. ■ Cover photo: Photolibrary

All illustrations by TRIGG

ABOUT THE SERIES

Culture shock is a state of disorientation that can come over anyone who has been thrust into unknown surroundings, away from one's comfort zone. *CultureShock!* is a series of trusted and reputed guides which has, for decades, been helping expatriates and long-term visitors to cushion the impact of culture shock whenever they move to a new country.

Written by people who have lived in the country and experienced culture shock themselves, the authors share all the information necessary for anyone to cope with these feelings of disorientation more effectively. The guides are written in a style that is easy to read and covers a range of topics that will arm readers with enough advice, hints and tips to make their lives as normal as possible again.

Each book is structured in the same manner. It begins with the first impressions that visitors will have of that city or country. To understand a culture, one must first understand the people—where they came from, who they are, the values and traditions they live by, as well as their customs and etiquette. This is covered in the first half of the book.

Then on with the practical aspects—how to settle in with the greatest of ease. Authors walk readers through topics such as how to find accommodation, get the utilities and telecommunications up and running, enrol the children in school and keep in the pink of health. But that's not all. Once the essentials are out of the way, venture out and try the food, enjoy more of the culture and travel to other areas. Then be immersed in the language of the country before discovering more about the business side of things.

To round off, snippets of basic information are offered before readers are 'tested' on customs and etiquette of the country. Useful words and phrases, a comprehensive resource guide and list of books for further research are also included for easy reference.

CONTENTS

INTRODUCTION

'Land of polluted river
Bloodshot eyes and sodden liver
Land of my heart forever
Scotland the brave'
—Billy Connolly
quoted in *The Big Yin* (1994) by Jonathan Margolis

ANOTHER BOOK ON SCOTLAND...

Welcome to yet another book on Scotland. So much has been written and rewritten on Scotland, Scottish life, its history and traditions that you might think that any author today would throw up his hands and say, "Enough is enough!" Yet somehow, Scotland continues to inspire fascination and love amongst visitors and inhabitants alike. Sir Walter Scott's 'land of brown heath and shaggy wood, land of the mountain and the flood' lives on in the hearts and imaginations of all those who go there.

This is a fine moment to take another look at a proud and increasingly confident people. After some three hundred years of political union with England, the Scots voted to have their own parliament in 1997.

The new millennium brought political devolution to Scotland with an elected assembly sitting in Edinburgh. Greater self-determination has inspired fresh hope and excitement in the country and its people

Scotland may remain part of Great Britain (England, Scotland, Wales and Northern Ireland), but it has always been a country apart. When you travel up from London on the train to Edinburgh or Glasgow, you don't need signposts to tell you that you have arrived in a different environment. In England, the countryside seems tempered and polished by time, the landscape neatly clipped and contained by centuries of overcrowding, over-farming and zealous gardening. In contrast, Scotland's rifts, faults and mountains seem to have been left in constant turmoil and revolt. The land and its people are truly different and in many ways seem rawer, younger and less cynical.

Some 80 per cent of the population live and work in the Central Belt, a broad swathe of land that takes in Edinburgh,

Glasgow and the 113 km (70 miles) or so in between. These two principal cities couldn't be more different. Edinburgh's stone facades, spires and gothic alleyways have an elegant if austere charm about them. Glasgow, one of the great cities of the colonial empire, weaves Old World grandeur into a modern day metropolis. The weather also distinguishes Scotland's twin urban centres. Edinburgh is airier, blown as it is by a cold wind from the east, while Glasgow catches the rain that sweeps in from the west.

While the cities and towns of the densely populated southern part of Scotland are important and wonderful in their different ways, it is the character of the land itself that has such a profound effect on people. Southern Scotland is an undulating territory of hills and river valleys separated by the cold waters of the Solway Firth. Once the centre of a strong textile industry, young people in the Borders, Dumfries and Galloway are now looking increasingly to the big cities for work.

Travel east out of Edinburgh and you're in the Kingdom of Fife, a peninsula of land running into the breakwaters of the North Sea with the town of St Andrews at its coastal tip. Although the landscape consists of flat and repetitive farmland compared to the Highlands, it still holds its own charm. Perhaps it's the string of old fishing villages that run all the way up to Wick in the north, a reminder of the days when the herring was king.

Travel up the coast and you'll reach Dundee and then Aberdeen. Aberdeen is the nation's third largest city and projects an oddly cosmopolitan image for a place so far north and so far away from the hub of things. Called the 'Silver City' by locals, fishing, in areas such as Stonehaven, as well as crude oil have brought prosperity and work to this windswept environment.

Drive inland from Aberdeenshire and you reach mountain country. In the mad dash up to Loch Ness and the Isle of Skye, many tourists miss out on the Central Grampians and Perthshire. This is Scotland's geographical hub, a huge area that takes in much of the Highlands and the Lowlands to the east and the west. The landscape is a fantastic mix of woodlands, deep valleys, rivers, high moors and mountains. In fact, there is everything here but the sea.

To the north, Inverness is a hard-bitten Highland capital that provides much needed service jobs and industry to the region. The surrounding countryside is breathtaking. Then, of course, there is Loch Ness itself, a lake so dark and deep that just looking at it sends a chill through you. There are many other places that most visitors never see. Hidden places like Glen Affric, where one of the last remnants of the old Caledonian forest can be found, or Loch Hourn, a spectacular sea loch situated on the west coast opposite Skye where the single track road ends at a tiny village.

Next to the far north, where cities and towns give way to narrow single track roads. It is here that you realise just how much of the country is open and uninhabited, one of the last wildernesses within Europe. Caithness in the North-east is a wide plain where the northern light takes hold and the skies and oceans start to dominate these thinning lands. Farming and fishing still cling on in Caithness, particularly in the aptly named town of Wick. During winter, daylight in this northern town feels about as short as the last flame from an exhausted candle.

Run on down the west coast from Sutherland through Kinross, Argyll and finally Ayrshire and you will see some of the most spectacular views in Scotland, where the mountains run into ocean and cloud, and sunlight and rain are constantly moving and mixing. This is also the heart of an older, rural Scotland, where salmon farming, shellfish and crofting provide much of the employment.

Scotland isn't just the mainland north of England, it is also a multitude of islands separated by the sea. There are about 800 islands dotted around the mainland, about 130 of which are inhabited. People living on these watery fringes still hold on to many of the country's traditions and dialects. Most of the Gaelic-speaking communities are on islands along the west coast such as Harris and Lewis. The islands off the north and east coast, such as Orkney and the Shetlands, are old Pictish and Viking centres. It's not surprising that the Scandinavians have had such an influence on these islands since Shetland is actually closer to Oslo than London.

Scotland is a country of contrasts, a country dominated by its landscape and its weather, an odd mix of old and new. Spend a day in Glasgow and you can buy top designer clothes, drink frothy cappuccinos, go to the theatre, eat anything from fish and chips to a Malaysian curry and dance the night away in a packed club. Travel 300 miles north and you are in the magical seascape of the Orkney Isles, where there are so few cars that pedestrian crossings were only introduced in 1999.

Many of the stereotypes about Scotland and the Scots contradict the modern reality. The Scotland in brochures and travel guides of castles, romance and battle sites means little to the majority of Scots who live in modern urban centres. Much of the big shipping and fishing industries of Scotland's proud industrial past have been reduced to old photos of stout men and women, baiting their long lines for the herring or beating out the vast steel bellies of ships.

Now in the spring of a political and cultural renaissance, the Scots are faced with the challenge of redefining themselves in the new millennium. Like the constant flow of weather and season in this magical northern land, the only certainty in Scotland is change. There couldn't be a more exciting time to come here.

A country as complex and multifaceted as Scotland cannot be squeezed into a single book, so I offer my apologies in advance for all the stories, places and people that I have been unable to include. They are still out there for you to meet and discover for yourself.

ACKNOWLEDGEMENTS

Thanks to Marcus, James, Maria, Dave, El, Suzie, Onya, Robin, Euan and Eveline—my friends and housemates by the Links. Special thanks to James for walking with me on a road less travelled, to Onya for her wicked turn of phrase and Marcus for keeping the humour flowing. I wish I could mention all the people who helped with my research but will have to settle for a special thanks to Paddy and Libby Shaw for their hospitality and wisdom, Penny Travlou for her insights and Roger Wood for getting me out of the rough. Thanks also to Nicolas Stepanopolus for giving me a place to rest on a long night and Jane and Ian for tying up loose ends with a few whiskies by the coal fire. Special thanks to Lucy, Charlie and Nigel as well as my new family, Roger, Jean and James. Love and kisses to my wife Fin, for being so unbelievably gorgeous.

To Simon Grant,
whose memory still walks the tops of Ben-y-Vrackie
on a bright spring morning.

Young girls dressed in traditional Scottish dress prepare for a dance performance at the Highland Games.

MAP OF SCOTLAND

ATLANTIC
OCEAN

ATLANTIC
OCEAN

SEA OF
HEBRIDES

SCOTLAND

NORTH SEA

EDINBURGH ●

NORTH CHANNEL

IRELAND

NORTHERN
IRELAND

ENGLAND

'O Caledonia!...
Land of brown heath and shaggy wood,
Land of the mountain and the flood,
Land of my sires!
What mortal hand can e'er untie the filial band,
That knits me to thy rugged strand!'
—Sir Walter Scott

SCOTLAND OBVIOUSLY LEFT Sir Walter Scott with a pretty good impression. But what does it do for the modern visitor, stepping for the first time off the train, plane or automobile into Caledonia? Does Scotland meet up to the often dizzy expectations heaped on it by the poetic ramblings of the likes of Scott and Robbie Burns?

A WEE NIP IN THE AIR

For many, the climate hits home before you even start to meet the people. Fly in under low cloud towards Edinburgh or Glasgow airports and the world below often seems cold, grey and windblown. Getting off the train in Scotland in the winter is like a military operation. Everyone in the carriage spends 5 minutes before the train arrives layering up with pullovers, jackets, bobble hats, scarfs and mittens. They step out of the carriage doors onto the platform as though parachuting from a plane at 30, 000 ft.

It isn't just the chilly airs that make their mark in Scotland. It is no exaggeration that you can experience four seasons in one day. The weather is as fickle as the sea that surrounds Britain, and a bright sunny day will as quickly turn to rain as a torrential downpour can suddenly lift and reveal a glorious, sun-lit rainbow.

Many first time visitors to Scotland are also impressed by the length of the summer days. In midsummer, a day of sightseeing can be an endless affair with as many as 16 hours of light to play with. I remember going to watch the sunset from a cliff top in the Shetland islands in July. We turned up at 8:00 pm expecting to be back in our hotel within a couple of hours. We waited and waited and waited until the sun finally sunk behind the horizon well past midnight.

A TRUE SCOTSMAN
At the end of the day, a country is defined by its people. Scots continue to enjoy a good reputation around the world and it is well founded. Most visitors are immediately impressed on arrival by how friendly everyone is. Compared to the English, Scottish people seem much more cheerful and relaxed. This is particularly evident in the countryside, where it is rude not to take time to chat to shopkeepers, the postman and even vague acquaintances you pass by on the street.

THE COUNTRY THAT TIME FORGOT
Many people who come to Scotland are immediately stunned by the wealth of history that virtually oozes out of the country's pores. Edinburgh seems like a gothic throwback to past times with its church spires, cobbles-stoned streets and granite terraces. Even Glasgow's contemporary big city buzz is offset by fading colonial grandeur. The city feels like a grand old dame with a story to tell on every street corner.

The countryside also resounds with the past. Whether it is the castles, graveyards and ancient *kirks* (churches) or far older standing stones and Pictic *brochs* (ancient stone structures), the bones of the country's archeological history are on full display. This unbroken link to ancient times can seem very exotic to visitors from countries such as North America.

BIG COUNTRY
Scotland's landscape deservedly makes a huge first impression on visitors. Drive or take the train up through the borders from England and the clutter of congested traffic and urban sprawl gives way to lush green hills and open countryside. Scotland feels like a frontier land from the outset.

Travel into the Highlands and the mix of *loch* (lake), moor and cloud-wrapped mountains—brooding sentinel giants bound by the roaring seas—is like something out of Tolkien's *Lord of the Rings*. At its heart lies some dark secret, barely concealed by a thin northern light. Even the bed-and-breakfast establishments are part of the same romance, with names like Rivendell and Saurian.

Outside of the towns and villages, the only company is wind, sea and stars. There are bars here covered with maps that chart the seas rather than the land, such is the ocean's dominance. On land, the place names—Cape Wrath, Loch Hope—indicate what a desperate act it must have been for those who first came to settle and invest in the place with their hopes and fears. Like Patagonia in South America, it feels as though you're about to step off the end of the world here, as though you are at some lingering way station between life and the supernatural beyond.

I remember walking along the shore at dusk one evening in Cape Wrath, on Scotland's most northerly coast. The waves on the beach were so high the whole sea seemed set to engulf us. We had crawled out onto slippery black rocks to look at a seal colony, lolling around on a flinty outcrop at the tide edge. They seemed unassailable there in their fat rolls of glossy skin. Behind, the flipper of a porpoise rose above the sea's heavy swell, white-tipped by the wind.

The waves broke over this northern isle, cloaked in mist and spread with seaweed, and a pair of dark ravens flapped like loose canvas in the cavernous skies overhead. We turned up our collars and squinted out at an inscrutable horizon beyond: Iceland, the Arctic, a mirror of ourselves. Most who visit Scotland get quickly acquainted with its Northern soul—elemental, timeless and unforgiving.

OVERVIEW OF THE LAND AND HISTORY

CHAPTER 2

'Work as if you live in the early days of a better nation.'
—Alasdair Gray, Scottish author

SCOT-LAND

Look at Scotland on a map and you wonder what all the fuss is about. Making up the northern region of the British Isles, Scotland stretches a mere 321 km (274 miles) from top to tail. Bounded by the North Atlantic to the west and the North Sea to the east, this ragtag straggle of land is dwarfed by ocean and the European continent beyond.

But what Scotland lacks in size it more than makes up for with sheer beauty. The mix of rugged landscape and shifting light draws photographers and painters from all over the world. In the south, the southern uplands are green fertile plains with rolling hills such as the Cheviots and rich pasture land on the lower slopes.

The central lowlands stretch from Firth of Forth in the east to the Firth of Clyde in the west. This is Scotland's engine house, brisling with urban centers, industry and the bulk of the population. It includes the country's two cultural centres, the capital Edinburgh and Glasgow, Scotland's largest city.

A single fault line that runs diagonally from Stonehaven in the East to Dunoon in the west neatly marks Scotland's northerly highlands and islands region. Here the softer, greener landscape gives way to a rough mix of mountains, lochs, bogs and heath. The highlands boasts the most dramatic of Scotland's scenery with mountain ranges of both sandstone and granite, rising 1343 m (4,406.2 ft) to Britain's highest mountain, Ben Nevis.

Wherever you are in Scotland, you are never far from the sea. Only 40 km (25 miles) wide at it narrowest point, Scotland has over 3,218 km (2,000 miles) of jagged coastline. This jumble of cliffs, white pearl beaches and salty fiords has been irresistible to travellers for centuries. There are also some 790 islands scattered around Scotland to explore, of which only around 130 are inhabited. The main groups of inhabited islands are the Inner and Outer Hebrides off the west coast and the Orkneys and Shetland isles to the northeast of the mainland.

Scotland's climate is as mixed as its scenery. Most people imagine that all it does in Scotland is rain. Rain is undoubtedly one of the countries guaranteed attractions. The comedian Billy Connolly spoke of meeting a tourist who said, "I went to Scotland and it rained." "Of course it rained!" was the reply. "What do you expect, the f****** Bahamas?" But there is also a lot more sunshine than most imagine, as well as considerable variety across the country. Broadly speaking, the west coast catches the worst of the precipitation. The east coast is dryer, brighter but often cold with a chilly North Sea breeze.

The other big variation is in the length of the days. In the summer, the countries' northern latitude means that sunset can be as late as 11:00 pm in the Shetland Islands. In the winter, the nights are, as the expression goes, 'fair draw in'. So much so that it can be virtually dark by as early as 3:30 pm.

The Gulf Stream affords Scotland a much warmer climate than it would otherwise enjoy. It still gets pretty chilly, with temperatures often dropping below zero in the winter. The summers are generally a few degrees cooler than England (expect an average of 19°C/66.2°F). Climate change has arguably brought milder winters in the past decade.

Statistically, your best chances of fine weather are in May, June and September. July and August are usually warm but may be wet and are the peak season for the dreaded midge, a small biting insect that favours boggy ground and unsuspecting tourists.

HISTORY

History plays an important part in attracting visitors from all around the world to Scotland. For many, the country's romantic image, carefully nurtured by its Tourist Board, sells the country and its people as a quaint tartan package. This image of 'heritage Scotland' is self-evident in any tourist shop along the Royal Mile in Edinburgh and now in most towns up and down the country. The image is of the picturesque Scotland of castles, kilts, whisky and of course the ubiquitous Loch Ness monster or 'Nessie', which is sold in all guises, colours and sizes—usually finished off with a tuft of ginger hair and a tartan cap.

The other common perception of Scotland is of Scotland the Brave, brilliantly characterised by the now legendary film *Braveheart*. In the film, a swashbuckling William Wallace (played by Mel Gibson) inflicts a series of crushing defeats on the English before coming to a sticky end. The real William Wallace ended up with his head on a spike on London Bridge, although the Scots have never lost his example of fighting spirit against the English.

As potent as these images of Scotland may be, they are more imagined than real. For anyone interested in Scotland and its people, disentangling the myth from the reality isn't easy. After all, myths are usually rooted in some truth.

The best place to start getting a better understanding of the Scots and their country is through their history—not as a dry narrative but as a story that begins and ends in the present, the 21st century.

The memory of a tartan army fighting off a numerically stronger foe still holds a lot of currency in Scotland. This unified face of the Scots still comes out in force on the international rugby or football field, usually painted blue and white for the colours of the Caledonian flag. Here they sing for their nation with a single voice, regardless of whether the day ends in victory or honorable and spirited defeat.

Early Days

The first clues to early Scottish history also lie in the landscape itself. As you travel through Scotland, you constantly come across signposts to the past. Driving just north of the border with England, across the narrow waist of Scotland between the Forth and the Clyde rivers, you'll pass the remains of the Antonine Wall. Completed by the Romans in AD 142, it became their first line of defense against incessant waves of attack from midges, rain and warring tribes to the north. In the end, the Romans beat a hasty retreat even further south, to Northumberland in England. Here they built the massive Hadrian's Wall and left Caledonia, or the 'land of woods' as they then called Scotland, to its own devices.

Roman remains are only a fraction of the story. Pushing north through Perthshire, a discerning eye can pick out prehistoric burial mounds and Iron Age hill forts dating from 500 BC. Inconspicuous village graveyards point to a past long abandoned by living memory. In the small village of Moulin, there is a 12th century crusader's grave, the outline of his double-handed broadsword chiseled into the stone. Whether he was one of the few crusaders who actually managed to fight their way into Jerusalem for Christianity only to be driven out by the Moors is lost to everything but the imagination.

Another graveyard, this time in the village of Meigle, is said to hold the mound and stone of Lady Guinevere of Arthurian legend. This is a somewhat dubious claim—there is little real evidence of King Arthur, his round table of chivalrous knights or his unfaithful wife.

The highland village of Glenelg boasts ancient stone structures known as *brochs*. These fortified dwellings were built by ancient Celtic settlers known as Picts. If you travel north to the Western Isles, you will find yourself in old Viking country, with the settlement remains of Jarlshof in Shetland and lurid Viking graffiti on the even older burial site of Maes Howe in Orkney.

In January and February, Shetlands locals still pay tribute to their Viking ancestors with two weeks of dancing and drinking in traditional pleated garb. Called the Up Helly Aa, this festival sees islanders marching through the town of Lerwick with torches and symbolically burning a mock-up of one of their ancestors' long ships.

Such remnants of Scotland's ancient settlers adds much to the country's mystique. The Pictish people were probably the

An old Pictish settlement or a *broch* near Glenelg on Scotland's west coast.

first inhabitants of Scotland and survived until the 8th or 9th centuries AD. All that we have left of them are the *brochs*, a few settlement remains and some wonderful carvings of both real and fanciful animals. The even older stone circles, such as Orkney's massive 'Ring of Brodgar', are a complete enigma.

From these pointers to early Scottish history, the immense diversity of cultures and peoples that lived there already contradicts the image projected today of a single, homogenous Scotland.

Whether it be medieval castles, Saxon hill forts, Pictish *brochs* or Viking place names, these signposts to the past tell not of one people but of many, all of them fighting to survive in an often inhospitable landscape.

The Scots

Scotland is named after, and peopled by 'the Scots'—the descendants of a number of different peoples long since conquered or assimilated. Looking back, the Scots' history and character seem etched in stone, but their ascendancy is far from certain. Scotland could have been called Pictland, Bretonland, Thorland or even England.

The Gaelic-speaking Scot actually originated in Ireland. Around 500 BC, they sailed across the Irish Sea and settled on the west coast of Scotland, mainly around Kinross, Oban and the Isle of Jura. From there, they spread along the west coast, introducing an early form of Christianity along the way. By the 9th century, their king Kenneth MacAlpine had merged the Pictish and Scottish kingdoms into one through conquest and marriage and called it 'Scotia'.

It is an amazing feat that the kingdom of Scotia actually survived the dark early Middle Ages. They were constantly under threat by Vikings raiding along the coast from their northern base in Orkney, as well as the Roman-Britons and the Anglos in the South. To the North, the Highlands remained impenetrable, filled with hostile and warring tribes. Internally, the kings were at loggerheads with feuding and ambitious noblemen.

Macbeth, Shakespeare's tale of murder and deceit, captures very well what must have been the mood of a time characterised by feuding, outright warfare and dynastic struggle. Such is the superstition that surrounds *Macbeth* that in theatres, it is only referred to as 'that Scottish play', to

avoid calling up its three witches with their boiling cauldron of bad luck.

The tale itself is based on real events. There was a Macbeth who ruled Scotia for 17 years after murdering the king, Duncan in 1040. Macbeth was himself killed by Duncan's son, Malcolm Canmore, in 1057 at Lumphanan near Aberdeen. Birnam Wood still stands outside Dunkeld. This is the same wood mentioned in Shakespeare's legend, which foretold of Macbeth's death by 'coming to Dunsinane'.

The lives of the early Scottish kings tended to be brutal and short and, most off them died with their boots on. But despite the kingdom's bloody ride through history, it did manage to survive, and by the 12th century had some semblance of unity and order. References to a Scottish parliament, with a body of recognised law and a system of judicial officers, called Judex dates back to the 12th century.

The Scots themselves didn't evolve from one ethnic group but from an enriched mixture of Scottie, Pict, Norman and Roman Briton with a dash of Viking blood. Looking at the Scottish people today, with their mix of dark-haired to blond to striking redhead looks, is evidence enough of this fascinating intermingling of peoples and destinies.

So the truth is that they are, and have always been, many different voices, and their ancestors were as often as not cutting each other's throats during the nation's tumultuous formation. But if the birth of Scotland had little to do with ethnic consistency or political stability, where does the Scots' sense of themselves as a single people come from?

The Auld Enemy

Scotland's long-standing opposition and resistance to the 'auld enemy'—the English—helped the country forge a clearer sense of itself as a distinct and independent nation. Ever since the first incursions by the Normans in the 12th century, the Scots have had to defend themselves from a numerically and economically stronger southern neighbour.

The Scottish peoples' resentment of their English neighbour is still palpable. There are certain pubs in the rougher areas of Edinburgh or Glasgow where it's best not to enter if you have an English accent. Every football or rugby match between England and Scotland is fiercely anticipated. Each victory by the Scots over the English on the playing field is like an act of revenge. Most Scots would rather support France or Germany when these countries play against England, instead of supporting the English.

This intense competitiveness and sense of common grievance has deep historical roots. As the historian George Mackay put it so succinctly, "No doubt it was in the logic of history that England would endeavour to absorb Scotland." The story of the Scots' early struggle to maintain their independence is an important one, as it set the pattern of Scottish resistance to English aggression that has echoed down the centuries.

The English king Edward I started the feud between the two nations after Scotland fell into civil war at the end of the 13th century. The Scottish king Alexander III died after a riding accident in 1286, leaving three rival claimants vying for the throne. Edward's attempts to 'unite' Scotland and England, first through marriage and then by brute force, drove such a deep thorn into Scottish-English relations that it was

to pitch the two nations into intermittent bloody warfare for the next three centuries.

Edward set up a nominal government north of the border under his control, enforced by an army that occupied most of the castles in the Scottish Lowlands. He even snatched the ultimate symbol of the Scots' political independence, the Stone of Destiny on which Scottish kings were traditionally invested, in Scone near Stirling. That the Stone of Destiny remained in Westminster for a further seven centuries, not to be returned to the Scots until 1996, is a good measure of England's desire for political hegemony over the whole island.

In the end, Edward and his son Edward II had bitten off more than they could chew. Led first by William Wallace and then Robert the Bruce, the Scots made an alliance with the French and rebelled. The country was plunged into a full-scale war of independence. For 30 years after 1285, the country's fate hung in the balance with the fortunes of both sides shifting between defeat and victory. The death of Edward I (known as the 'Hammer of the Scots') in 1307, combined with Robert the Bruce's relentless guerrilla warfare from the Highlands, decided matters in favour of Scotland.

Robert the Bruce defeated an English army of up to 100,000 soldiers at the battle of Bannockburn in 1314. This resounding victory, one of the few decisive moments in Scottish history, paved the way for the formal recognition of Scottish independence at the treaty of Northampton in 1328.

Of course this wasn't the end. Rather, it set a pattern of English ambition and aggression in Scotland, countered by Scottish attempts to hold them off, even turning to France to even up the odds. The English and Scots continued to raid and kill each other across the borderland of the Southern Lowlands for centuries. The term 'bereaved' comes from the Selkirk Reivers who were infamous for their bloody sorties into northern England. If you were 'reived', you were certain to be bereaved. This area still has the desolate feel of a no man's land, a buffer zone between two hostile people whose history and land is stained with spilt blood.

Scotland did finally end up in a union with England, first through inheritance, when the Scottish King James VI inherited the English throne after the death of Queen Elizabeth in 1603, becoming James I of England. In 1707, under Anne of Orange, the Union of the Crown made the two countries effectively one.

The End of Clan Independence

Most Scots still have the old clan names, such as MacGregor or MacDuff, but the Highlanders of *Braveheart* fame have long since moved on.

The clans were tribes of people, bonded by blood and land, who lived and fought together under a single family name. Fiercely independent, each clan answered solely to their chief (or laird), and spent more time quarrelling with their neighbours than taking on the English. They were entirely self-sufficient, living off their own crops, game and Highland cattle, often raided from their neighbours.

This clan system of local autonomy only survived into the 18th century, as the Highlands were too inaccessible for laws, kings and tax collectors to make any lasting impression. However, sooner or later, the growth of the nation state, coupled with boundless imperial progress, was going to come up against this ragtag army of feudal tribesmen who didn't want to pay homage to any leader but their own.

That moment came with decisive brutality in the summer of 1746 when the highland clans, led by Bonnie Prince Charlie, were defeated at the battle of Culloden.

Prince Charles Edward Stuart (also called Bonnie Prince Charlie, or the Young Pretender) was the last in a long line of Scottish Stuart princes who tried to reclaim the English throne by raising invading armies in the Highlands.

The Stuarts were Scotland's, and arguably England's, rightful kings. James Stuart I of England, who was also James Stuart VI of Scotland, succeeded Elizabeth I and governed the whole island with little opposition from 1603. However, James' son Charles I and his grandson Charles II were both arrogant and ineffectual rulers. For a start, they were Catholics in a predominantly Protestant state. To make matters worse, they espoused the divine right of kings to absolute power, putting them at odds with the nobles in parliament who wanted more say in government. Charles I ended up being beheaded at the hands of Cromwell in 1640, and his son James II was deposed by the Dutch protestant William of Orange in 1688.

These Stuart kings may not have had the Highlander's best interests at heart, but from exile in France, they were quick to exploit support in the far north for their claim to the English crown, which was known as the Jacobite cause. Resentment toward the union of the crowns, and with it the loss of Scottish sovereignty in 1709, had promoted a string of failed Jacobite rebellions before Charles made his reckless bid for power in 1745.

Charles' support was always much patchier than is commonly imagined. If the whole of the Highlands had marched to his banner, the historian John Prebble estimates that he could have raised 63,000 men, easily enough to march all the way into London. Internal rivalry and division meant that there were never more than 5,000 to 6,000 on the march at one time.

They still came close to toppling King George I, who was a German from the Hanovarian line, from the English throne. Prince Charles' army made it as far south as Derby in England in December 1745. King George was so worried that he was prepared to flee the country had the Highland army marched on London. Instead they retreated, giving George time to regroup and, at the hands of his son the Duke of Cumberland, inflicting a final solution on the restless natives of the north.

The defining moment for the fate of the Highlands came on a boggy area of ground called Drummossie Moor at Culloden outside Inverness. It was there the English forces, better fed and equipped and greater in number, met a demoralised and exhausted Highland army on 16 April 1746.

The site of the battle at Culloden, which is now a popular visitors' centre, has an eerie feel to it. The mass graves of the fallen clansmen are marked with small headstones, and legend has it that heather never grows on these grassy mounds. The battleground flutters with flags marking the positions of the two armies before the Highlanders' desperate charge. It is hard to imagine that the course of so much history could have been channelled into such a narrow patch of desolate moor.

The Highlanders' charge that day, their only battle tactic, fell short on the flat ground against a barrage of musket and cannon fire. Bonnie Prince Charlie, whose poor military planning had caused the massacre, fled a field spilt with the blood and hopes of a generation of clansmen. As well as the estimated 1,000 killed on Culloden moor, some 1,150 were shipped abroad and countless others executed in the weeks that followed the battle.

The Highlanders were loyal to their prince to the very last. Bonnie Prince Charlie is still remembered in story and song as the noble hero, fleeing capture by the English forces across the Highlands. He managed to escape back to France from the Isle of Skye, disguised in the clothes of the young Scottish woman, Flora MacDonald.

The Clearances

The real story is in what happened after Charlie left. In a series of punitive laws passed by the parliament in the years following the rebellion, known as the Concessions of the Act of Union, the Highland way of life and culture was brutally suppressed. Wearing tartan, speaking Gaelic or even playing the bagpipes was banned. Land owned by anyone who had supported the Jacobite cause was confiscated. Army barracks, some still standing as bleak ruins to this day, were erected outside communities to house government troops in case of further trouble. The old clan ways were effectively outlawed.

With the collapse of the clan structure in the aftermath of Culloden, clan chiefs or lairds increasingly played the role of traditional landlords, exploiting the people on their lands rather than protecting them. They chose to fill their glens with the far more profitable Cheviot and black-faced sheep rather than people. Termed 'the Clearances', thousands of poor tenant farmers were forcibly evicted and herded into boats bound for the colonies from the 1840s to the 1860s. The sheep that replaced them were nicknamed four-footed clansmen, since there were so few actual clansmen and women left.

Blaming the emptying out of the Highlands in the 19th century on greedy landlords alone is short of the whole picture however. Many chose to leave, unable to manage even subsistence farming because of the poor soil, especially when there were plenty of jobs in the new industries in the cities.

But that thousands were rounded up and exported is beyond dispute. Many deserted glens with the remains of old stone homesteads are a legacy of the Clearances. I remember exploring the old crofts behind our cottage, abandoned since the owners were evicted over 150 years ago. The remains of an old pot and some utensils were still buried in the hearth of the fire. Whoever was there couldn't have had time to take anything with them; they were simply dragged out and marched onto the waiting boats for the New World. Sometimes their homes were burnt behind them.

Regret over the loss of the old Highland way of life can be compared to modern attitudes about the lost cultures of the Native Americans. Both peoples have since been immortalised as a symbol of a way of living the modern industrial world has lost. The clans of the Highlands will always be romanticised, seen through the coloured lenses of regret for a vanished world, like the fading paintings of tartan-clad men fighting to their last breath on Culloden Moor.

Rule Britannia

Although it's tempting to portray Scotland as one of history's underdogs, this is far from the truth. Scotland is still a part of Great Britain and has been for three centuries now. For the most part, that time has been successful, with the two 'rivals' benefiting immensely from economic and political inter-dependence.

Political union with England in 1707 brought new opportunities for Scotland, as the Scots themselves were very quick to realise. The 18th and 19th centuries were a time of smug progress for the Scottish Lowlands, as industrialisation and trade made the country increasingly affluent and self-confident.

Entrepreneurial in spirit and quick to seize upon new technological advances, the cities became centres for the production of linen, cotton, wool, paper, coal and iron.

From Edinburgh and Glasgow, merchants traded these raw materials for luxuries such as tobacco, tea and opium from countries as far-flung as Egypt, North America, India and Turkey. Many grew incredibly rich in the process.

The affluence of the 19th century can be seen in Edinburgh's New Town, with its towering streets of grey stone Georgian and Victorian houses, complete with Doric pillar entrances and sweeping cast iron staircases. Glasgow boasts the famous architect Charles Rennie Macintosh's visual feasts such as the Art College, which puts to shame the cheerless concrete shoeboxes many 20th century buildings resemble.

Such was Edinburgh's feeling of self-importance during colonial times that the residents built a huge Roman-style acropolis in Calton Hill to the west of Princes Street, and dubbed the capital 'the Athens of the North'! Blackened by petrol fumes, the monument has lost some of its colonial grandeur and is now a gay cruising area, as well as a seasonal focal point for pagan rituals ushering in the summer or winter.

The Scots themselves became great travellers. In service of the empire, many were posted overseas—in particular to India and South Africa—as missionaries, soldiers, administrators or explorers. David Livingstone (1813–1873), the most famous of Scottish explorers, mapped out large areas of Africa only to be eventually swallowed up by it.

Nowadays, hoards of young people still take off with a backpack and a traveller's journal to map out their own journeys of self-discovery. They tramp around far-flung destinations such as Australia, the Far East and America, often living on a shoestring and following the maxim that the greater the hardship and adventure, the more authentic the experience.

Many of these travellers are following in the footsteps of their forefathers. In the 19th century, many without a viable future in Scotland left and travelled to the ends of the earth in search of frontiers where land and opportunity could be found. Rural poverty in the Highlands, and the landlords' zeal to introduce sheep into their lands, forced many abroad. New colonies established in North America, Australia and New Zealand benefited immensely from these hardy and tenacious settlers. The place-names in these distant lands

I remember reaching the last farm on the mainland of Southern Patagonia in Argentina to be greeted by a tall red-headed man in cowboy chaps and a chequered shirt. He told me in impeccable English how his great-grandfather had travelled to Argentina from Scotland in the 1860s, marked out the land he needed, built a house and started rearing sheep. The original house still stands and little has changed since. His extended family exports wool across the globe and still maintains strong links with the old country in both language and customs.

bare witness to how homesick the settlers were, often naming them after the places they had left behind. For example, there are places named Glenelg in every one of these countries.

The huge numbers of Scottish people who fled their homeland over the past two centuries go a long way towards explaining the peculiar nostalgic romance that Scotland holds in the hearts of so many. The land itself is dramatic and beautiful. The fact that so many Scots went unwillingly has made them regret leaving Scotland even more. Perhaps all that homesick dreaming has conjured up an imagined Scotland. No wonder there are so many companies offering to trace genealogies for distant clan relatives.

Empire Ups and Downs

As Scotland took to the seas, it became an international centre for shipbuilding. From the 1840s, Aberdeen was building the tall sailing ships, or clippers, that chased the tradewinds around the world, competing with America in the Chinese opium trade. With the invention of steam engines and iron-hulled boats, the Clyde River in Glasgow and to a lesser extent Leith docks in Edinburgh became the centres of the Scottish shipping industry. In 1870, the Clyde docks employed 20,000 men and Scotland produced 70 per cent of the iron-hulled ships launched in Britain.

The Age of Empire brought with it the era of 'Scottish Enlightenment', a time of great advances in science and the arts. To mention a few famous names, there was James Watt, inventor of a more efficient steam engine, and Alexander Bell, who devised the first telephone. There were also several famous thinkers, notably the geographer James Hutton, philosopher David Hume and economist Adam Smith.

By the end of the 18th century, Scottish doctors had made such a reputation for themselves that they were in demand across Europe. The Russian Tsars, Peter the Great and Alexander I, as well as Catherine II, all had Scottish physicians. Most famed of them all was Sir James Young Simpson, who discovered chloroform. Such was the general flowering of the time that Voltaire once quipped, "At the present time, it is from Scotland we receive rules of taste in all the arts."

As much as this period of British history glitters for Scotland, it did not come without cost. The philosophy of economic laissez faire, in which the individual pursuit of maximum economic reward was expected to somehow benefit all, ended up benefiting the few. In the 18th century, Scotland became an increasingly urban society as thousands abandoned their fields in search of work in the big industries in the South. City life often brought untold misery to the thousands who came in search of that ever elusive better life.

Cripplingly low wages at the looms, pits and shipyards made Scottish industries profitable but left a lasting legacy of urban deprivation. With an inadequate diet and cramped living conditions—whole families often shared a single room—diseases such as smallpox, consumption, fever and 'bowel hives' took a terrible toll. Infant mortality rates during this period speak for themselves. An examination of 1,508 deaths in the city parish of Glasgow in 1791 revealed that 694 of those were under the age of two. Until 1850, half of all those who died in Glasgow were under the age of 10!

The old town in Edinburgh was so disease-infested that much of it was finally sealed off and eventually rebuilt. However, the smart new Georgian buildings, called the New Town, were no less forgiving to the city's underprivileged. The grand steps that run up to the front entrance disguise the basements from which the landed, professional and merchant classes were served. A whole army of scullery maids, kitchen maids, parlor maids, table maids, lady's maids, housekeepers, cooks, footmen, valets and butlers served and lived under their masters in the main house.

These divisions, despite a large and affluent middle class, are still evident in the enormous gap between rich and poor, with low wages barely sustaining large sectors of the economy. In recent years, for example, a proliferation of call centers for businesses and services have sprung up, made profitable by low wages, long hours and very limited union protection. The fact that low-income people are still crammed into council estates on the outskirts of towns is rarely commented on. The 19th century system of exploitation—justified by those great Victorian landmarks of 'progress', empire and industrialisation—has made such levels of poverty an accepted part of reality to this day.

Scotland's participation as part of Great Britain and the empire went largely unquestioned throughout the 19th century and survived two world wars. This shared history brought with it a common identity and being British still holds considerable currency amongst older generations of Scots. Many Scots who remember World War Two and the hard years of rationing afterwards have a clear sense of nationality, considering themselves first to be British and only secondly Scottish.

This has as much to do with World Wars One and Two as with the memory of empire. The Scots, Welsh, Irish and English stood and fought as one in both wars. They shed the same blood and still rub shoulders, albeit in graves and memorials. Their sacrifice in the defense of Great Britain is a shared one.

Mind you, that doesn't mean you can confuse a Scot with an Englishman without getting a few sharp words in reply. Much like the Canadians' prickly relations with their neighbours to the south, it's best not to jump in and say, "So you're from England," when you meet someone from Britain until you're sure they are truly 'English'. However, for someone from the British Isles to say that they're from Britain, rather than Northern Ireland, England, Scotland or Wales, is still common.

In many ways, it's a noble sentiment. Feeling part of a union of differing nations, whether it is Great Britain, the former Yugoslavia or Europe, allows for greater cooperation and dampens the ugly side of nationalism: xenophobia and racism.

However, that sentiment is fast fading amongst the younger generations. For Scots in their twenties and thirties, being British seems increasingly irrelevant these days. As the MSP for the Scottish Nationalist Party Alistair Allen told me, "People who don't have a recollection of empire, or crucially the Second World War, really have very little notion of what Britishness is."

'D' is for Devolution

In June 1999, after three hundred years of Scotland being ruled from London, Scotland's own parliament was officially opened by the Queen in Edinburgh. This immensely symbolic moment was the culmination of a century of struggle in Scotland for greater political autonomy.

By the early 20th century, the glories of empire had started to lose their sheen for Scotland. Competition from countries with even cheaper labour costs helped make the big labour intensive industries such as iron and cotton increasingly unproductive. But rising unemployment was only part of the story.

The First World War decimated a generation of men and punctured the confidence that so many had held in the logic of Empire and the inevitability of progress. Europe had proved itself to be as much a centre for barbarism as a centre for the spread of 'civilisation' to dependant states. By the 1930s, unemployment exceeded 20 per cent in Scotland and Soviet Bolshevism was on the march in Clydeside.

The Second World War brought a brief Indian summer on the economic front, with a revival in demand for the big ships of trade and war, bringing money to the docks and yards of Aberdeen, Glasgow and Edinburgh. But the writing was on the wall—Scotland increasingly became a poor hinterland to the financial and consumer boom in the south-east of England. With the axing of many rail lines and bus routes in Scotland after the Beeching Report in 1963, the country's disappearance into a northern isolation seemed complete.

With Scotland's economy controlled from Westminster and practically no political say on the domestic or international stage, the country might have seemed to have quietly slipped off the world map. The North of England, synonymous to most southerners with darkness, poverty and deprivation, could have extended all the way to John O'Groats, and Scotland the nation could have been left to the memory of history books and old wives' tales.

But in the end, there was too much to Scotland; it was too distinct and proud to give up so easily. As well as the Scots' strong sense of themselves as being culturally distinct from the English, the original 1707 Act of Union with England allowed Scotland to keep its own practices in law and education, which it has done ever since. Scotland has clung to its sense of individual and separate identity with continued tenacity.

The Scottish National Party first found a real voice in Scottish hearts from the late 1960s with its calls for independence. The discovery of oil—dubbed 'black gold' by locals—177 km (110 miles) off the coast of Aberdeen in October 1970 suddenly made the idea of political independence an economic reality for the Scots. It was just a matter of time before the old drums of resistance to rule from the south started beating again.

For the two main parties in Britain—the Conservatives and Labour—full independence has always been out of the question. However, the idea of some level of regional devolution for Scotland and Wales has been batted about since the early 1970s. In 1979, the Labour Party took the country to the brink with a referendum for devolution. Although 51.6 per cent voted 'yes', it was deemed inconclusive. It would be Scotland's last chance to have a say on the matter for another 18 years.

Ask the Scots what made it obvious to them that they needed their own parliament again and they'll most likely reply, "Margaret Thatcher". Although the 'iron lady' kept up her support in England throughout the 1980s, the Scots never had much time for her. In 1988, the height of her political fortunes in England, Scottish football supporters showed her a sea of red cards and practically whistled her out of the national stadium at Hampden Park when she made a rare visit north of the border. They spoke as a nation increasingly beleaguered by rising unemployment and neglect from Westminster.

Thatcher's commitment to open market economics did not protect Scotland's ailing industries. The textile, shipping and coal industries collapsed as Scotland shed a third of its jobs between 1979 and 1981. The Conservatives showed little interest in Scotland, confident their popularity in the south would outweigh poor showings in Scotland.

Soaring unemployment in the 1980s and 1990s brought a new face to Scotland: desperation, drug abuse and a prevailing sense of hopelessness. This was the Scotland depicted in the film *Trainspotting*, where directionless youths stumbled from one heroin fix to another and then into crime to pay for their habit. This scale of drug abuse has largely declined since the early 1990s.

When Scotland finally had another say over the question of devolution after a landslide victory by the 'new' Labour Party in 1997, they didn't falter. In the referendum held on 11 September 1997, an overwhelming majority of 74.3 per cent of the nation voted for devolution and 63.5 per cent voted for tax-raising powers. Scotland had gone full circle, building a new and daringly modern parliament opposite the site of the old one in Holyrood Palace.

THE SCOTTISH PARLIAMENT

Thankfully, the change to Scotland's political landscape has been much further reaching than the flash new parliament building, completed in 2004 around £ 100 million over budget. Scotland's political representatives, known as MSPs, are elected under a system of proportional representation. This is a big divergence from traditional British politics where the party that gets the most votes in national elections wins office. The 'first past the post' policy often ends in a predictable confrontation between the two big hitters, Labour and Conservative, with little real say from the smaller parties on the fringes.

In contrast, proportional representation in Scotland encourages a more consensual style of politics. Proportional representation is an electoral system in which each political party is represented in a government according to its actual voting strength in the electorate. Win 60 per cent of the vote and you get 60 per cent of the seats. This forces parties to work together to find common ground and ensures that smaller parties and interest groups have a say in the decision-making process.

Although the Scottish Government has suffered its fair share of scandal and criticism, devolution in Scotland has proved to be a success. With Wales and Northern Ireland also moving towards greater political autonomy, this could be the beginning of a new federal Britain, rather than power remaining centred in London.

'I' IS FOR INDEPENDENCE

For many, and in particular the Scottish Nationalist Party (SNP), devolution is not enough. The argument goes that if Scotland is to truly grasp its own destiny, nothing less than full independence is enough. This logic holds some weight; parliament in Westminster still reserves judgment over big matters such as energy, foreign policy, defense, social security and broadcasting. The Scottish parliament's survival is still dependent on Westminster, the British State can still dissolve Scotland's fragile federalism any time it wishes.

Moreover, the say that Scotland has in Europe is still very limited compared to other even smaller independent states such as Denmark or Luxembourg. To avoid slipping back into the parochialism and isolation of the 1970s, nationalists claim that Scotland needs a full say amongst the member states of the European Union and NATO. Critics of independence argue that Scotland is too small to support itself economically without financial support from London. The old debate continues...

FLAGS AND ANTHEMS

The flag of Scotland—a white diagonal cross on a blue field—is called a Saltire. It symbolises St Andrew, the patron saint of Scotland. The Saltire was first said to have appeared in the sky to the Pictish King Hungus before he trounced the Anglo-Saxons at the battle of Aethelstaneford. It has been used as a symbol for the struggle of independence since the middle of the 14th century.

The national flag of the United Kingdom—the Union Jack— also flies in Scotland. The flag combines the cross of St George, the patron saint of England with the cross of St Andrews and a cross similar to Ireland's patron, St Patrick.

The official national anthem throughout the UK remains 'God Save the Queen'. However, the Scottish have adopted 'Flower of Scotland', 'Scotland the Brave' and William Jackson's 'Land of Light' as their own anthems. Another sentimental favourite is Robert Burns' 'Auld Lang Syne', traditionally sung over New Year Hogmanay celebrations. At sporting events, especially rugby internationals, Scottish fans fly the blue and white Saltire flag and sing 'Flower of Scotland'.

RELIGION

The established church in Scotland is the Protestant Church of Scotland. It is also the largest with over two million members. The Roman Catholic Church is another major presence, mainly due to successive waves of Irish Immigrants in previous centuries.

Catholics and Protestants have been at each other's throats since the reformation in the 17th century. This is still mirrored in sectarian tensions in the south-west of Scotland, although it is largely played out amicably on the football pitch between the countries biggest teams—Celtic and Rangers

Religion used to play a seminal role in Scottish society. In the 18th century, the Presbyterian Church, or *Kirk*, had a say in most aspects of public and private life.

Amongst older people and in the more isolated areas of Scotland, the Free Church, or 'Wee Free', as well as other Christian denominations, still hold a lot of sway.

The Free Church is a peculiarly Scottish form of Presbyterianism, closer to Calvinism in its Puritan zeal. Nowhere is its control over public life more evident than during Sundays, known as 'the Sabbath'. The Sabbath is a day of rest in respect for God's work. That means you can't garden, book into a hotel or even put your washing out. Even the ferry doesn't run to the islands of Harris and Lewis on a Sunday.

In recent years, a growing immigrant population has brought a rich diversity of religions and creeds. Religions such as Islam and Buddhism are now well represented in the bigger towns and cities.

Although religious education is still compulsory in school, the idea of going to church on a Sunday has lost much its appeal in an increasingly secular society. Young people are more likely to turn to non-conventional sources of spiritual 'new age' wisdom, if they take an interest in religion at all.

THE SCOTS

CHAPTER 3

'As Dr Johnson never said,
"Is there any Scotsman without charm?" '
—Sir J M Barrie, British novelist, author and playwright,
in an address to Edinburgh University

POPULAR SCOTTISH STEREOTYPES

Trying to tease a 'national character' out of the Scots is not easy. For every supposed character trait, there are a thousand exceptions and many of the stereotypes are far from consistent. The Scots are portrayed as being open-hearted and generous, courageous, tightfisted and dour, high-spirited and cynical—all at the same time. Drawing a clear thread through all these supposed traits and characteristics is impossible. The best course of action is to take all generalisations with a healthy pinch of salt.

Part of the difficulty lies in presuming the Scots to be one people, one unified 'type'. The Scots are just as clearly marked by their differences as their similarities.

They come together to pour scorn on the English or celebrate a national sporting victory, but they are also divided by class, geography and prejudice—some as deep as the fault lines that run through the country itself. So any Northern exposure can only be skin deep—a cursory look at some of the similarities and contradictions that make up the Scottish people, bonded as they are by the same history, language and salty land.

Open and Friendly Folks

Watch an old black-and-white war film and you will invariably see English, Welsh and Scots soldiers bunkered up together on a front line, united in their animosity toward the Germans.

The Scot, often called Jimmy, bubbles with chatty exuberance. His English and Welsh companions are usually more circumspect, displaying a stoic reserve under fire.

This is a classic image of the Scot, upbeat and full of easy banter. It is also pretty accurate. Most travellers who visit Scotland comment on how friendly the people are. Whether buying something in a shop or just waiting for a bus, it's easy to slip into conversation with locals. Scots love to chat, and will pass comment on pretty much anything. They are a friendly and approachable people and nowhere is this more evident than in Glasgow.

Wander around Glasgow and you would think you were in a small village rather than a big city—so many people have the time to stop and exchange a few friendly words. This is a marked difference from southern England where reserve and tact rule the day. The trend in Britain is that the further north you go, the warmer the people tend do be, in inverse relation to the climate.

To Be Tight

England is awash with jokes about the Scots' legendary frugality, most of them as tired and hackneyed as the jibes about the Irish being stupid (which also couldn't be further from the truth). One of the few half-decent jokes is of an Englishman and a Scotsman in a pub together. The Englishman spots a fly in his beer and, complaining bitterly, demands a new pint from the barman. The Scotsman likewise sees a fly in his drink, gingerly picks it out of the froth and holding it in front of his face by the legs hisses, "Spit it out you wee bastard."

The Scots themselves are happy to have a laugh at their famed meanness with money, although Aberdeen usually seems to come out worst. A common joke in Glasgow is that if you knock on someone's door at teatime (dinner) in Glasgow, the host will invite you in saying, "Come in and have your tea." If you do the same in Edinburgh, they'll say, "Oh, you'll have had your tea." In Aberdeen, you'll be presented a wonderful spread of food and drink, laid out on the dining room table—with a price tag neatly attached to everything.

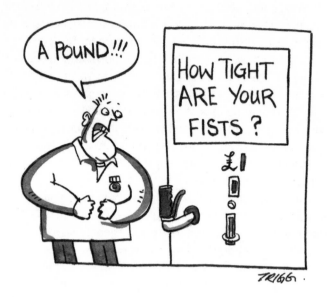

The image of the Scots being tight may be a source of mirth on both sides of the border, but it's best not to take these jokes too seriously. With Scotland having been a poor relation to much of Western Europe for centuries, its people are accustomed to being prudent with money. I know two Scots brothers who are so conscientious of their expenditure that it looks like they are pulling teeth rather than pound coins every time they open their skinny wallets.

However, when it comes to hospitality—to friends or strangers alike—money doesn't enter the equation. The Scots are equally famed for their open-hearted generosity. Get invited over for a meal and every effort is made to prepare a generous spread. It's almost rude not to accept second helpings. Likewise in a bar, if you get chatting to a stranger, they will include you in a round of drinks, even if they're down to their last pennies.

Spirited Warriors

Scotland is a small nation with a big heart, or so the story goes. The image of the Scots beating back their brutish

English neighbour is an enduring one. It has generated an imagined landscape of Scotland the brave, a united warlike people fighting off a far greater foe.

Such is the romance of this image that there is a whole society called Clan Wallace that carry on the clansmen's cause. They dress up in tartan, wearing T-shirts with slogans like 'Kill more with a claymore', and ride around hanging tough on motorbikes. Together they supply the demand for wild and hairy Scotsmen in films such as *Ivanhoe* and *Braveheart*. But the Scots' tenacious spirit isn't just re-enacted in films. At international sporting events, especially rugby, the Scots genuinely come together to cheer their nation on in a single voice. Players and fans put in 110 per cent commitment, whoever the opponent and whatever the odds are against them.

There is nothing to match the atmosphere in Murrayfield Stadium in Edinburgh at a 'six nations' rugby match, when the Scots urge their team to yet another Herculean effort. It was like that in February 2006 when Scotland wrestled a grand slam victory from England and broke a six-year losing streak against their greatest of opponents.

Facing an English team buoyant after beating France, Ireland and Italy, only the weather added an element of chance to what seemed a foregone conclusion. The rain came down in torrents, and seemed to sweep the players and the whole pitch into a grey oblivion. The rain switched to hail and some 60,000 Scots sung on their team in the wintry downpour. In the end, Scotland won 19–13 and whether or not you like rugby, you simply had to admire their victory. Through sheer strength-of-spirit the Scottish team had outplayed a stronger opponent.

That the Scots are a proud and nationalistic people is beyond doubt. Whether sporting performances such as these draw on a national tendency of fierce warlike resilience in the face of adversity is another question. American immigrant Pearson Fernside who has lived in Scotland for five years seems to think so. He explained, "The Scots are a decent, hardy and tenacious people who tend to drink too much."

The Hard Man

The image of Scotland as a nation of spirited warriors is a little one-sided. After all, it's hard to be one of those sporran-swinging clansmen, or rugby players battling on the field, if you're a woman. Scotland is something of a macho society, where the hard man still cuts a provocative swagger across the nation's collective psyche.

Try and imagine prominent Scottish women who stand out as emblematic symbols of Scottish history or contemporary culture. Flora MacDonald and Mary Queen of Scots jump immediately to mind, after that it all gets a bit thin on the ground.

In contrast, there are a whole host of Scotsmen famed for one enduring feat or another: James VI of Scotland for becoming king of England, David Livingstone for finding Victoria Falls before getting lost, Sean Connery for being Sean Connery... the list is endless.

It isn't just that men have got the lion's share of the press in Scotland. The famous ones are usually loveable rogues—macho, gritty and never too far from a fight. Some of the first Scottish 'big men' to make names for themselves were, oddly enough, saints. Around the 6th century, the legend of St Columba who came to Scotland from Ireland to convert the pagans to Christianity is far from being a story of a peaceful monk. He is said to have taken to the woods to single-handedly slay wolves and wild boars to prove his manhood.

Scottish male heroes have been living and dying by the sword ever since the beginning of history, and probably before. Just watch a James Bond film with Sean Connery and see the 20th century idol of many Scots—a dashing and ruthless womaniser with nothing to loose. Robert Carlyle's terrifying 'Begsby' from the movie *Trainspotting* also plays out a more contemporary version of this rough and uncompromising spirit. Characters like Begsby also point to a dark underbelly of frustration and violence in Scotland, tucked away from prying eyes by the best work of the Scottish Tourist Board.

Quick Witted

The Scots are known abroad for their sense of humour. This is hardly surprising given that one of their greatest ambassadors overseas, Billy Connolly, is a comedian. Billy Connolly—or the Big Yin as they call him in his hometown of Glasgow— now lives and works in America. But his humour remains an enduring example of Scottish wit at its sharpest—fast, irreverent and self-deprecating.

Billy Connolly comes from a long line of Scottish jokers to hit the stage or television screens in the last century. They date back to the old music hall comedians such as Stanley Baxter and Sir Harry Lauder. They played drunken hard men even when sober, men with sharp tongues and sentimental hearts. Glasgow was always a great one for pantomimes; the sound of the boos and hisses of the audiences would carry for streets around the theatres that they were held in.

Some of the best comedy still comes out of Glasgow, most notably the television series *Rab C. Nesbitt* and *Chewin' the Fat*. The humour in Ian Patterson's screenplay character Rab C Nesbitt borders on self-hate; the ramblings of a beer-touting working-class guy whose stream of broad Scots speech needed subtitles to be understood properly in England. He represents a grimmer reality to Glasgow, where poverty and desperation (as well as humour) is a part of many people's lives. Rab is the reeling, swearing contradiction to the Glasgow of boutiques and European coffee shops that just will not go away.

There was one old boy on the west coast who lived in a caravan and made his living from telling jokes and stories to passing tourists. He would wander down to the local bar, groomed to perfection in a tweed suit, tie and hat. There he would weave fantastic stories to appreciative tourists who would buy him drinks and food in return. And so he survived for many years, never, or so they say, telling the same story twice.

Humour is not reserved for the professional comedians in Scotland. Pretty much anyone can hold an audience, tell a great story and get a good laugh at the end of it. In most areas of Scotland, a fast wit is revered. At school, you can be a stunted child with specs and still command the respect of the big lads if you can cut them down with a few quick words (and survive the beating).

Dour

Bizarrely, Scots are considered to be dour—serious, cynical and downbeat—as well as high-spirited and funny. The old black-and-white version of the classic film *The Thirty-Nine Steps* has a typical portrayal of the dour Scotsman. The dashing young hero takes refuge in an old farmhouse in the Highlands whilst fleeing from the police. The farmer is a long-faced cantankerous old character that lives a meagre existence of hard work and self-discipline. His wife, however, is young, beautiful and lonely; I needn't tell you the rest.

This image may not do the Scots any favours, but it does have a historical basis. While the English took on the Protestant Reformation in the 16th century half-heartedly, in Scotland, Calvinism swept the country and the Church, or Kirk, took a keen interest in all aspects of social custom. Pleasures such as dancing, singing and sex outside of marriage were effectively banned in place of a life of simple austerity and hard, honest work.

Although the days of supremacy of the Kirk are long over in all but the most isolated communities, the stereotype of the dour Scotsman or woman is a hangover from those times. Older 'God-fearing' Scots can still have a certain severity to them. One friend's father who is a retired minister used to ask him every evening when he was a boy, "Well son, what have you done today to justify your existence?"

DIVIDED WE STAND

I stopped to chat with a homeless man on the street one day. He asked me if I was a student before ranting against all students, barely drawing breath between invectives. A man in a big car with a suit caught his eye and he moved on to rich people, saying they were all snobs and middle class bastards who only cared about their cheque books. Next came the English: "Soft southern losers the lot of them," he spat. I wanted to ask him if there was anyone he didn't hate, but thought better of it.

Everything is not as it seems in Scotland. Despite the country's popular image as a hospitable and peaceable nation, like anywhere else in the world, there is plenty of room for hatred and prejudice. In defining the Scots, it is just as important to look at their differences as well as their similarities.

Rich and Poor

Pass through Edinburgh and Glasgow and you can't help but be impressed. Edinburgh's city centre—Princess Gardens, the Castle and the Royal Mile—are breathtaking. Glasgow has less of the old stone facades but more of the frenetic big city vibe with its big glass buildings, art galleries and boutiques. Visit some of the residential areas close to the centre and the picture is complete. Affluent areas such as Bearsden in Glasgow and Morningside in Edinburgh, with their smart cars and well-clipped gardens, point to a wealthy and contented society. Although the affluent middle class is real in Scotland, it's a mistake to think that this is the norm.

In part it's a clever illusion; a thinly painted veneer of Georgian grandeur laid on for residents and visitors alike. Behind those impressive streets, the cities have a darker story to tell, a story of poverty, drug abuse and neglect. Housed in decaying government-built 'housing estates'—either tenement flats or high-rise blocks—Scotland's urban poor have little in the way of work, education or hope. Most of the estates they live in are tucked out of sight and out of mind.

Glasgow has the most visible problems, dating back to the days of the Industrial Revolution when thousands were crammed into single room tenement buildings to work in the factories and yards. In rougher areas in the east and north of the city—such as Easterhouse and Possil—the only substantive change nowadays is that most of the industry that once sustained these populations has dropped away, leaving a legacy of unemployment, desperation and alcohol or drug abuse. There are thought to be upwards of 10,000 heroin users alone in Glasgow, the highest concentration in Britain.

Poverty and decay in one of the worst housing estates in Glasgow.

The story is a similar one in cities and towns across Scotland. The poorer areas of Edinburgh are a long, long way from the grandeur of the New Town.

Ben, aged 19, who lives in the Wester Hales estate, said, "It's about survival. There's no proper heating in the flat and I live on the ninth floor, so I have to board up the windows every winter to stop the wind blowing them in."

Aberdeen is no exception, 'boasting' one of the highest gaps between rich and poor in Great Britain. With no real political will to address these vast inequalities in Scottish society, the Scotland of Irvine Welsh's *Trainspotting* looks set to endure. As the Society of Gal-Gael, concerned with urban regeneration, puts it, "The culture of Scotland, so rich in Celtic, Pict and Norse traditions, has been reduced to tourist clichés, whilst mass unemployment, inner city urban decay and social alienation have produced a culture of dependency, drug addiction and violence."

Many Scots live in gritty urban environments, making few trips into the countryside that makes their nation so famous. In the film *Trainspotting*, Renton and his pals take a break from their drug-frenzied lives in Edinburgh to go for a walk in the country. On arrival in the big outdoors, they wander around confused and disorientated before returning to the familiarity of their granite jungle.

There is also a broad gulf of experience between those who grow up in the country and those from the cities. Several community projects are working to bring these two worlds together. For example, the Camas project set up by the Iona Community brings children from deprived and inner city backgrounds to some old fishing cottages on the island of Mull. There they spend up to two weeks walking along the coast, abseiling off cliffs and gardening.

Camas' director Rachel McCann told me, "It's a real culture shock for the kids when they first come here, one boy didn't even know that chips come from potatoes. But by the end of their stay, none of them want to leave."

Class System

The class system is one of Britain's trademarks, an unwritten social hierarchy that has been established over several centuries. Although it may not be so readily apparent to the outsider, most people in Scotland belong to a particular social class, however much they might prefer to deny it.

British society is roughly divided into three classes. The working classes are traditionally poorer, disadvantaged and work in areas such as industry, skilled labour and trades. The middle classes, who represent a wide range of people, are better educated, wealthier and tend to take on professions such as medicine and law. The upper classes, aristocracy or 'blue blood' as they are occasionally termed, aren't always rich, but have millennias of privilege to keep them at the top of the heap.

This is only a thumbnail sketch and there are plenty of rebels, exceptions and anomalies but it does give some idea of the broad divisions that exist in Scottish society. The clearest marker is schooling.

Children who are sent to private schools (confusingly called public schools) tend to be from upper-middle class or upper class families. Children sent to state schools are more likely to be from lower-middle or lower

Lucy Grant, an American who has lived in both Scotland and England for over 25 years, swears that her status as a foreigner has been socially advantageous. Unable to place her, the British are forced to take her as she is rather than box her into a class and judge her by that.

classes. However, it's also much more complex than that. The area you live in, your accent, dress sense and even your diet all serve to 'class-ify' you.

Common to all class consciousness are varying degrees of misunderstanding and snobbery. Just as a labourer will sneer at someone with a public school accent, so the middle classes can look down on the working classes with a mix of disdain and fear. It's often easier to be a total outsider.

Protestant and Catholic

On the west coast of Scotland and especially in and around Glasgow, there is a strong 'sectarian divide' between Protestants and Catholics. Although nominally about religion, in reality, this division runs much deeper than just which church people attend on a Sunday. It ties into history, identity and soccer. Sectarianism is so deeply embedded in some areas that, like the ongoing 'troubles' in Northern Ireland, there seems little way out of an impasse that defies the logic of negotiation.

The confrontation between Catholics and Protestants dates back to the potato famine in Ireland in the 1840s. Unable to survive in Ireland, tens of thousands of poor Irish immigrants came to the west coast of Scotland in search of work. Such a large influx of Irish Catholics was quickly seen as a threat to the Protestant Scottish community. Before long, whole communities in Glasgow were divided along national and religious lines. Today, the distinction between Irish and Scottish has long since blurred but the memory of mutual resentment and religious intolerance has endured.

In Northern Ireland, these sectarian divisions still rage on in the streets, but in Scotland, they are largely confined to the football pitch. Football in Glasgow is much more than a spectator sport. It is an all-consuming passion that encompasses sport, religion and ultimately politics. It is hardly surprising that Glasgow is the only city in Europe that houses three 50,000 plus capacity football stadiums—Ibrox, Celtic Park and Hampden Park.

The two biggest football clubs in Scotland, Rangers and Celtic, mirror the sectarian divide. Rangers' fans come predominantly from the Protestant community and Celtic fans are mostly drawn from the Catholic community.

The two camps of supporters are incredibly loyal and devoted to their respective teams. Team colours, white and green for Celtic and blue for Rangers, are worn with swaggering pride. For many, a loss on the football pitch is taken as a personal blow; success is met with jubilation bordering on hysteria.

Both Celtic and Rangers clubs have non-sectarian policies but their supporters are under no illusions. Such is the animosity between the two sides that 20 years ago, pitched battles raged in the stands and even on the pitch itself. These days, violence is usually limited to verbal abuse but the centre of Glasgow is still a virtual no-go area the night after a Rangers-Celtic match. Many of the pubs bar anyone wearing team colours to avoid trouble. For soccer fans who want no part of this collective insanity, there is always Partick Thistle, whose Protestant and Catholic patrons stay clear of the sectarian divide.

This ancient confrontation between Catholics and Protestants peaks in and around Glasgow with the Orange March on 12 July. This is when members of the Protestant 'Orange Order' march through the streets to symbolically assert their authority over the Catholic community. There is seldom any violence but as the procession marches through Catholic areas, you can cut the atmosphere with a knife.

The march, repeated across Northern Ireland, reasserts a cycle of resentment and violence that seems inexhaustible. A friend told me once how he saw grown men on an Orange march in Lanark hurl verbal abuse at a passing child of six or seven just because he was wearing a Celtic football top.

Highlanders vs Lowlanders

Geography has always divided Scotland and its inhabitants. The Lowlands, that broad swath of agricultural land that makes up Southern Scotland, supports the bulk of the population. Better connected by land and sea, the Lowlands have been the centre of the industrial revolution, cultural expression and political representation in Scotland for centuries.

In contrast, the Highlands have remained on the margin, stubbornly independent and considered for centuries a savage backwater. Fear and loathing has traditionally cut both ways. In the past, Highlanders have been quick to write off Lowlanders as soft anglophiles who had lost touch with their Celtic roots. The old resentments still linger in some areas, where someone from the south can still be termed a 'Sassenach', a derogatory Gaelic term for a lowlander.

The east and west of Scotland is also divided by old rivalry. The two principle cities are forever competing for political and cultural ascendance. Most Glaswegians would prefer the new parliament and the capital city to be in their hometown. Likewise, folk from Edinburgh secretly wish their city had a bit more of Glasgow's buzz.

Jealousies such as these are light-hearted and make for plenty of jokes and comparisons. People from Edinburgh usually end up being portrayed as being cold and arrogant or 'snooty' and the Glaswegians as being just plain mad, or 'mental'. The rivalries don't end there. Traditionally, there is little love lost between Glaswegians and Aberdonians, although I have no idea why. Perhaps this once tribal society has just always needed a neighbour to compete with.

I remember watching the weather forecast one evening on the television. The map of southern Scotland flicked up with its usual mix of little rain clouds and suns. Only there was something missing—Edinburgh. Instead of placing the capital city on the map, the nearby towns of Haddington and Kirkcaldy were clearly marked. The most logical explanation is that the programme's producers are based in Glasgow and someone there would rather forget that Edinburgh ever existed!

SO WHAT MAKES THEM TICK?

Scottish people avoid neat definition. Perhaps the one quality that draws these people and all their contradictions together is their setting. An island people, often cut off from the rest of the world by mountains or sea, they have learned to be resourceful, independent and sometimes circumspect. As a result, they admire free thinkers, especially those with a sharp sense of humor. Scots don't tend not to suffer fools gladly and can be quick to speak their minds.

Scottish people have a well-deserved reputation for hospitality. They are usually charming to strangers, although they can take excessive interest in other peoples affairs. They place great value on friendship, but can be initially hard to get close to. Reserved when it comes to personal matters they rarely talk openly about their private lifes.

The Protestant work ethic is hard wired though their veins and they respect education, hard work and an entrepreneurial spirit. However, no matter how reserved or serious they may seem, scratch the surface and they are wild at heart. The Scots take great pride in their country, but their true loyalties lie with their local community, friends and family.

TRADITIONS

Traditions that are unique to Scotland have often survived the country's pagan past. The best known is Hogmanay. Originally an old Celtic festival to ward of evil spirits and hasten back the sun with huge bonfires, Hogmanay is now a massive knees-up held to usher in the New Year.

In the countryside, homes are thrown open and the first visitor, or 'first foot', across the door of a friend's house after the beginning of the New Year is celebrated with a drink of whisky all round. This tradition is most prevalent in the smaller communities, where a whole village circulates from one home to the next having an alcoholic drink in each until the early hours and often days beyond.

I once went round to visit the Kennedy family a few days after the New Year in Perthshire. John Kennedy asked me if I would like a drink and I said I'd love a cup of tea. "Would you like a drink with your cup of tea?" came the reply.

In the towns and cities, you can drop by at most parties regardless of whether or not you know anyone and expect a warm welcome. It is also tradition to kiss anybody of the opposite sex that you happen to bump into, so remember to take lots of lip balm. It is a wonderful, open-hearted and joyful celebration.

Although Hogmanay is technically just the one night of celebration, it generally turns into a two-week binge of eating and drinking from Christmas until around 6 January. When folk get tired of the theme of ushering in the New Year, they carry right on celebrating just for the sake of it. The only way to get through such sustained festivities is to stay on the alcohol, a steady flow to hold off the hangover till you make it back to the normal world again.

Halloween

Halloween is another tradition in Scotland that has retained a distinctive pagan slant. 31 October is the night before the old church festival of All Hallows, or All Saints' Day. This is also an important date in the Celtic calendar, Samhuinn the Feast of the Dead, during which spirits are said to come back to haunt the living. Samhuinn holds more appeal with the young who hollow out pumpkins, cut with grotesque faces to scare away the dead.

Witches were said to be very active during Samhuinn. They still are, in the form of kids that go out dressed up as ghouls, witches and apparitions to demand sweets from their neighbours. Called trick-or-treating elsewhere in the world, it's called *guising* in Scotland. Originally, the *guisers* had to sing or recite a poem to earn their reward of sweets, but now the costumes are enough. The trick, such as a fireworks through the letterbox, can be real if people are unfriendly and don't hand over sweets.

Burns Night

On 25 January, most households celebrate the life and times of Scotland's principal bard (poet). The poet Robert Burns has an enduring reputation in Scotland. An instinctive rebel just when the French Revolution was throwing over the old guard, he brought a breath of fresh air to the stifling social constraints of late 18th century. With a swashbuckling, boozing lifestyle and breathtaking skill with words—he is reputed to have written the famous poem 'Tam O'Shanter' in a day—Burns has captured the popular imagination ever since.

Burns Night is a social occasion, when friends gather to eat *haggis* (the famous Scottish dish), *tatties* (potatoes) and *neeps* (turnips) and drink a *wee dram* (a small drink of spirits) or two to Burns' dear departed ghost. The night is also filled with ritual. The *haggis* is traditionally brought to the table accompanied by a piper playing traditional tunes on the bagpipes, where Burns' 'An Ode to the Haggis' is read out to much applause.

After the meal, it is time for the speeches. 'The Immortal Memory' is the most important attempt to eulogise Burns' life and achievements. There is much room for interpretation here as little is actually known about the man himself. The male guests are also given free reign to compose a 'Tribute to the Lassie', and the women then come up with the 'Lassies' Reply'. These poems certainly lack the lyricism of Robbie Burns and are often smutty and raucous. Not that Burns would have minded—he is known to have been a veritable Don Juan of the north himself.

The form speeches take is far from rigid. The 'Tribute to the Lassie' can be a tribute to almost anything. I have heard tributes to agriculture and whisky. At the Burns Night held by the Scottish Labour Party, satirical poems were scribed for both the parliament in Westminster and the new Edinburgh equivalent.

Although many celebrate Burns Night in Scotland, the romance of the night holds a stronger pull outside the country. In North America, the tradition has really taken off amongst the country's Celtic descendants. Clubs such as the well-to-do Caledonian Club in New York hold huge society dinners with upwards of two hundred guests. Even the desert state of Nevada, a far cry from the rainswept mountains of the Highlands, boasts a Cold Country Celtic Society. The society holds a huge party complete with pipers, Scottish dancing and a free bar (unheard of in Scotland) on the night of the 25th.

In London or New York, the pubs and bars often give out *haggis* and whisky on Burns Night as the Scots émigrés or their descendants reminisce about their old country. In the bars of the main cities in Scotland, it's business as usual and the dinners themselves tend to be much more intimate affairs of family and friends. However, this doesn't mean that Burns is forgotten.

Storytelling

A rich tradition of oral storytelling survives in Scotland from ancient Caledonian times. Scotland abounds with tall tales that were first told as ballads or song—poems later came to furnish the imaginations of some of Scotland's finest writers. Scots still love a good story well told and storytelling festivals are still held throughout Scotland.

As a result, the country is so steeped in myth, legend, ghosts and superstitions that if you delve too deeply into it, the shadows can start playing tricks on your eyes. Witches are only one of the myriad of fairies, devils, brownies and other mythical creatures that have been dreamt up or reportedly seen in Scotland. Many are a mix of old Celtic and Norse legend, and this is not surprising for an island people intimately related to the sea. It isn't just mermaids that lure sailors into their watery paradise. The big grey seals that live off the shores have long been associated with the mythical *selkies* (meaning seals in Orcadian dialect), that occasionally come onto land and assume human form. No one agrees about whether they are fallen angels or humans cast out for previous sins. If you get a chance to watch seals draw near you in the *gloaming* (dusk) with their large liquid eyes gazing at you curiously across the water, you may find the old legend taking on fresh life.

FITTING IN

CHAPTER 4

'May the best ye've ever seen
Be the worst ye ever see.'
—Traditional toast

PACE OF LIFE

To those used to the hustle of a big metropolis, Scotland's principal urban sprawls can take a little getting used to. The nation's capital Edinburgh is a good example. Coming from the mad rush of London, Edinburgh has a flavour not unlike a small town in Spain or Italy. Life is much more laid back. In the summers, the meadows in the parks are filled with sun worshippers, amateur footballers, frisbee fanatics and the unfortunates who have to make it to work but don't seem in any particular hurry to get there.

In the winters, the Scots settle into the long cold nights and short cold days with ease. Like a squirrel in winter's icy grip, they also seem to retreat into semi-hibernation. The windswept streets become places to dash along between work, home, a bar or a crowded café. In London or New York, a café is a place to snatch a cappuccino before appointments, or just to be seen with your designer clothes, sunglasses and mobile phone. In Edinburgh or Glasgow, café life is about relaxing, chatting with friends or whiling away an afternoon with a book and your own thoughts. Outside of the cities and towns, life is even more relaxed.

PERCEPTIONS OF STRANGERS

Scots are used to seeing tourists from all round the world and in all shapes and sizes. Visitors to the country should therefore expect a big friendly welcome rather than fear or mistrust.

Coming from big multicultural centres such as London or New York, Scotland can seem very 'white' to outsiders, but this is changing fast. Nowhere is this more evident than in Glasgow, where there is a growing Asian community. The old stereotype of the pale Scotsman or woman is breaking down. Nowadays in Glasgow, you're just as likely to see a woman of Indian descent, dressed in a sari saying 'Hiya' in a thick Glaswegian accent.

MANNERS
Mind your Ps and Qs
Being polite is very important in Scotland. The Scots pride themselves on their hospitality and friendliness, and are generally cautious and respectful of their fellow human beings. 'Please', 'thanks pal' and 'sorry' punctuate most conversations. If you bump into someone, it's likely that they will fire off an apology before you do.

A reputation for good manners is common to the British Isles. While people in the south of England can be very courteous, they can lack the sincerity of the good-humoured friendliness of the Scots. At least that is the perception of Penny Travlou, a Greek national who has lived in both England and Scotland over the past six years. "I think that the Southerners (from southern England) are polite without meaning it, but the Scots really do mean it," she said.

Just Say No
The British in general and the Scots in particular find it hard to say a direct 'no'. If asked a favour, they will say 'maybe' even when they would rather not. This inability to say 'no' is most common with invitations. Few will initially turn down an invite, be it for a party or a holiday. Only later, they may end up making their excuses or just not turning up. Generally they didn't change their mind, they just didn't want to offend in the first place.

In general, the Scots and the British are also quick to make vague promises to 'come round', 'get together' or 'see you tomorrow' before quickly forgetting about it. This is just a polite way of saying 'goodbye' and can be very confusing to the unsuspecting foreigner. I had one poor German friend who actually waited in for a couple of weeks because some people she met had said they would 'pop round to visit soon'. They never showed.

The trick is managing to tell when 'yes' actually means 'probably not' and when agreeing to meet again ('See you soon') is actually a polite way of saying 'Goodbye for now'. Classic phrases that say 'yes' but usually mean the opposite are: 'Oh aye, that sounds nice,' or 'That sounds interesting,' or 'I'll have to think about it.' The Scots, masters of understatement when they want to be, will often damn an idea or project with faint praise rather than condemn it to your face.

Public Reserve, Private Space

The Scots are at heart a reserved people. As friendly as they may be to strangers, it takes time to get beyond the banter and make genuine friends. Penny Travlou saw this odd contradiction first hand when she came from Greece to live in Glasgow. "Glasgow still has something of a community feel to it," she told me. "If you wait at a bus stop, someone will definitely talk to you...But my biggest frustration when I first came was making friends."

Penny found that it was harder to gain the trust and confidence of Scottish people compared to those in Greece. "In Greece, you can meet people and socialise with them easily, but it doesn't mean that they will become close friends...here people need time to feel relaxed and comfortable with you, but once you get to know them, they make excellent friends," she said.

This reserve is most evident when it comes to the home. 'Home is where the heart is' goes that most overused of British expressions. It's a cliché because it is so true. Just look at the energy put into most gardens in Scotland or leaf through an *Ideal Homes* magazine and you get some idea of the love, care and attention that most put into their living spaces.

Someone's home is an intimate and very private expression of himself or herself. So it's best not to pop round to someone's house or flat without an invitation if you don't know them too well. "It's strange, home is a private castle here," says Penny. "When I first came, I used to drop in on people uninvited and feel like I was invading, now I phone beforehand to give some warning."

Talking About the Weather

The weather in Britain is an obsession. You only have to listen to Radio 4's *Shipping Forecast* to get a sense of the place the weather has in the heart of the British nation. The names listed in the forecast circling the coast of Britain are timeless and unchanging. Delivered in a clipped English accent, the voice is soothing even when it warns of gales and storms.

The best icebreaker in most conversations is to pass a comment on the weather. It's a way of making an extended 'hello' and it oils the wheels of social interaction. Since the weather is so unpredictable, there is always something new to remark on.

For example, much like the Arctic Inuit people's 100 names for snow, the Scots have a myriad of different ways of describing their national affliction: rain. It can be raining, showering, pissing it down, pouring, spitting, drizzling, misty or just a wee bit wet. Perhaps only a native would be able to differentiate between 'Showers sometimes heavy' and 'Persistent rain'.

The next best bet to commenting on the weather is to make a feeble attempt at the impossible—a prediction. Actually how accurate you are is irrelevant, it's more about making the right noises.

Coping With the Weather

Talking about the weather in Scotland is the easy part, you then have to survive it. Amber from Australia lived through a winter in Dundee dreaming of surfing the waves on the beaches outside her hometown of Sydney. "I missed the heat back home so much," she told me, "there were days when the wind was so strong that I used to just scream at it with frustration."

If you're from a hot country, the weather can take time to adapt to. My Spanish friend Nacho complained that it isn't the winters that are so bad, he expected them to be long and dark. It was the cool damp summers that followed after he had survived the winter that he found the hardest.

Spring can be the cruellest. In March, the daffodils push themselves reluctantly out of the soil, the cherry trees burst into bloom and there is the first whiff of cut grass as lawn mowers get dusted off to trim long dormant lawns. Days lengthen, the sun pops out and you can be forgiven for breathing a deep sigh of relief and rejoicing that spring is here—at last.

Don't bet on it though. As often as not, the winds and cold return their icy grip overnight, throwing the country back into winter for a spell. It's as though the god of weather is one of those dour Presbyterian ministers who frowns on anything less than hard work and suffering. "Aye well you've had your fun, now that's it! Get back inside and back to work, your punishment isn't over yet you bunch of snivelling sinners!"

However, the weather isn't as bad as you may have been led to believe. Scotland suffers from the many myths of a cold country. Nacho was told before he arrived that if the curtain touched the window during a Scottish winter, it would freeze and break off. He arrived in December to be pleasantly surprised at how mild it was compared to his dire expectations.

There is also more sun around than you might expect. On a hot day in southern Scotland, the thermometer can peak at 30°C (86°F). A common complaint further north is that the weather forecasters constantly leave a dark cloud hovering over them on the map, even when it's a beautiful sunny day.

There is also a real magic to the weather's capricious turns. A day can start with rain, turn to hail, snow and sleet before brightening up for a glorious afternoon. One friend reasons that the weather goes a long way toward explaining the Scots' ingenuity and quick wit. Constantly kept on their toes by the continual swing of the barometer, they adopt something of its fast-moving spirit.

Dress Sense

Dress sense in Scotland is far from exotic. Little thought is given to style outside of large urban areas, where young people in particular sport designer wear. In most of Scotland, the dress code is pretty flexible, depending of course on the weather. The notable exception is the club scene when sleek young things dress in the finest fashions. Older people take more care with their appearance and tend to be well turned-out in neat, if a little sombre, attire.

Oddly enough, this lack of attention to what you are wearing can be refreshing, particularly for people from countries like Italy or Spain, where so much time is spent in front of the mirror. Penny is thankful, "The Scottish can be terrible dressers with no sense of fitting things together, but on the other hand you feel more comfortable here. You can dress casually and you don't have to wake up in the morning and say, 'Oh my God what am I going to wear!'" she said.

Tartan Times

Traditional Scottish dress is more and more in vogue, especially with young people. Scotland's trademark, the tartan, is worn at weddings, funerals, Highland balls, posh nights out and sometimes just for a few beers in the local pub. The tartan is made up from different coloured yarns and woven together to produce a multicoloured check, called a 'sett'. Each clan name has a number of distinctive patterns or setts to choose from.

It is only since the 17th century that specific tartans have been reserved for family names or clans. But the tartan has been an inseparable part of Highland dress for centuries. Look at the colours of the Highlands in any season and you will understand where much of the inspiration comes from. In the autumn for example, the stag grass seems on fire in deep orange, the bracken beside it is a rich rusty brown and the Rowan tree berries add a bright splash of red.

The colours once came from the very plants they reflected. There are hundreds of plants that give good colour in Scotland. Some of the most important are the lichens, which give a wide range of rusty oranges, as well as rich purple

Father and son team up in tartan.

when soaked in ammonia (urine!). The myrtle provides deep greens, iris gives black and yellow can be made from many plants.

Technically, it is only fitting to wear tartan if you have a clan surname, either on your mother or your father's side. However, if you can't claim clan ancestry, do not despair.

Since most patterns are relatively recent inventions, you can always invent your own. For example, the racehorse Red Rum had his own tartan made especially for him.

Tartan is most typically worn as a kilt. The kilt, based on the premise that knees are an erogenous zone, needs no introduction. Legend has it that nothing is ever worn underneath a kilt, although the cold, midges and a revealing spin at a *ceilidh* can make for strong disincentives. Other options are the drainpipe tartan trousers or 'trews' for men and a tartan sash worn over an evening dress for the ladies.

Kilts aren't cheap to have made up, costing around £ 300 each. But they are a lifetime investment, with a few extra inches measured into the girth for lateral growth in years to come. It is possible to rent kilts, although it is hard to find the lesser-known tartans. Most Scots have their own kilts made up and rent the rest of the clobber for around £ 40 a night. This includes a tweed or Argyll jacket for casual wear or a smart Prince Charlie jacket for more formal occasions. There is the ubiquitous leather pouch or sporran round the midriff, coming in all shapes, sizes and with all variety of animal hairs. Footwear is a pair of distinctive ghillie brogues and long socks with a small black knife, known by its Gaelic name of '*sgian dubh*'.

GOING OUT
Drinking
In Britain, drinking to excess is not only acceptable amongst the young, it is virtually expected of young men. If you go to a bar and drink nothing but Coca Cola through the night, you'll be met with mild disapproval. Real men and women are supposed to drink beer after beer from pint glasses. This is often topped off by a bruising round of spirits.

Compared to Mediterranean countries which mix dancing, eating and drinking in even measure, Britain has much more of a beer culture. Drinks are often bought in rounds, so if you go out as a group everyone is expected to buy everyone else a drink at some point. Over the course of an evening, this can all add up to a lot of alcohol and it's not uncommon to see men and women staggering home blind drunk and in full song at the end of a night out.

Drinking in Scotland

Dimitris came to Edinburgh to study at the Herriot Watt University for three years. Born and raised on the island of Corfu, he knew something of the British drinking culture from seeing the yearly invasions of holidaying Britons to his island in the summers. He didn't think much of their habit of getting steamingly drunk and collapsing on the beaches every night. But he thought they were just letting off steam while on holiday

On moving to Scotland to study, he was surprised to discover that the British habit of drinking to drunken excess isn't reserved for holidays. He saw the same spectacle of staggering groups spilling out of one bar or another on a Friday or Saturday night, barely able to make their way home.

"In Greece," Dimitris told me, "drinking that much is frowned upon. It's not acceptable to lose control like that and make such a fool of yourself."

Flirting

Flirting is in some ways a much subtler affair in Scotland than in many other cultures. Men in particular tend to be shy when it comes to approaching, or 'chatting up' a woman. Penny comes from Greece where men are much more direct, and is often confused. "Men can be shy and have this terrible fear of rejection," she told me. "You don't have any idea how someone feels about you and end up trying to guess." Whereas in countries such as Italy, it is understood that men will make comments about women in the street; in Scotland, it's a privilege reserved for workmen.

Alcohol loosens tongues and gives men and women an excuse to relax and flirt. Scots are much more forward when they are drunk. They can have a one-night stand and justify it as, 'Oh I was drunk' the next morning. There is a strong sense of monogamy within relationships, and although affairs happen, they are less socially acceptable than in some other cultures.

A Note on Saunas

If you're in Edinburgh and fancy a quick sauna to ease the cold from your joints, think twice. Most saunas are fronts for brothels. Although it's officially illegal to run brothels in Scotland, in Edinburgh, the police turn a blind eye, reasoning that it's safer for all concerned to keep the oldest of professions behind closed doors. Elsewhere in Scotland, prostitutes remain on the streets.

This can lead to confusion if caught unawares. Jeannine came over to stay from France and saw a job advertisement for a 'sauna assistant', in the local paper. Thinking that it would mean showing clients around and keeping the place neat and tidy, she called up to inquire. The owner got very excited when he heard her French accent on the phone and asked her for her height and vital statistics. Confused, Jeannine asked just what the job entailed as it hadn't been very specific in the advertisement. "Oh," the man replied, "just massage and a little extra." She hung up.

KEY RITUALS
Growing Up
The major birthdays in the passage to adulthood occur at the ages of 18 and 21. They are usually big celebrations and often come with big presents from the parents, such as a first car or a crate of expensive wine that has been put aside for years to mark the occasion.

For those who make it, graduation from university is also a seminal moment in most young adults' lives. It marks the end of student life and entry into the world of work. Graduation is a matter of pride for the whole family, and it is common to see portraits in living rooms of sons or daughters on graduation day, together with their beaming parents.

Tying the Knot
Marriage, that most ancient of social institutions, is still respected in Scotland and remains one of life's important rites of passage for many. I know from experience that there is nothing more nerve-wracking and exhilarating than going down on bended knee to ask a girl for her hand in marriage.

Customs are changing however, and there are many couples in Scotland who prefer to marry late, or not at all. According to the Office of National Statistics, the number of single and never-married thirty-somethings in Britain rose from 969,900 in 1987 to 2.3 million in 1997. Cohabitation is more common as many people are put off by high divorce rates, now running higher than one in three in Britain.

To become legally married, you have to have your names recorded in the civil registrar. This is available at a civil registration office, a church or pretty much anywhere you like, provided there is a minister present. Once the marriage is legally recorded, the ceremony that follows is entirely a matter of choice. The ceremony can be Catholic, Protestant, Hindu or pagan. You can get hitched in a mosque, in the botanical gardens or naked on a beach, although the climate is likely to make this last option too bracing an experience. Most choose to get married in a church.

The party afterwards is called a reception and is generally held in a country house, the town hall, or a huge tent or marquee in the parents' garden. Historic Scotland does a roaring trade in hiring out castles and old stately homes for weddings and receptions. Demand for most big venues is high, especially during the marriage season between March and October. So bookings have to be made up to a year in advance.

In Edinburgh, a common choice is a civil service or reception at the city council building. High up on the sixth floor, guests can look out over the nearby folly of stone and spire—the Caledonian Hotel—and to the Forth River's meeting with the sea beyond. But there is little time to reflect on the view. Arriving from the church, the guests are generally keen to get down to the highlight of the wedding: the fabulous party after the ceremony.

They are seldom disappointed. No holds are barred in providing plenty for all at the dinner and dance after the wedding. The event tends to kick off with tall glasses of champagne to loosen the guests' reserve. Guests are seated at tables set with linen and silver, waiters hover and all await the entry of the bride and bridegroom. The master of ceremonies, usually a man but not the bride's father, announces their arrival and the hall erupts into cheers and applause as the couple breeze in.

Seated at a long high table, the first round of wine is served to them and everyone has to wait for the bride and bridegroom to start each new course. The food is most commonly a buffet, usually with a wide choice of cold and hot foods including luxuries such as lobster, prawns and even caviar laid out on sumptuous platters.

With the serving of dessert, the wine is finished and the glasses replenished with champagne. This is followed by the speeches. The master of ceremonies leads this long-winded, often drink-sozzled and sometimes embarrassing series of speeches and minor confessions. The keynote speech is the best man's. This is when the best friend of the bridegroom pulls a series of well-rehearsed skeletons out of the closet, retelling some of the more embarrassing moments in the bridegroom's life.

This can touch on anything from his dress sense in the old school days, his desperate antics as a single man and, of course, how he fell hopelessly in love with the bride. These can be tense moments for a bridegroom as he hopes the booze and the limelight don't go to his friend's head and his speech fall on the wrong side of discretion. The meal ends with the cutting of the wedding cake, usually a heavy fruitcake in an elaborate multi-tiered design.

Having survived all this consumption and socialising, everyone is then expected to loosen their belts and dance until the early hours. The bride and bridegroom start the dancing off with a solo number, to a few shed tears in the audience. Then everyone old and young alike joins in. The younger legs dance reels until the early hours.

The finale of a Scottish wedding is often the most revealing. With the drink finally taking its toll and most feeling exhausted from the day's hectic proceedings, people tend to drop their guard. The two families either hit it off really well, or can rub each other the wrong way, fostering grudges for years to come. Singles often make a play for a partner in the reception's last hours and many a fresh romance blossoms. It is commonly joked that the bridesmaids are guaranteed a *snog* (kiss).

Some time toward dawn, everyone says their goodbyes and makes their way back to their hotel rooms none the wiser but one hell of a lot fuller than they had been the day before. The bride and bridegroom summon their last energies for the wedding night and the waiters eat the leftovers in the back kitchens.

All that's left is the colossal bill for the event, which can run into tens of thousands of pounds. It is traditionally the responsibility of the parents of the bride, with the exception of the drinks which can be paid for by the bridegroom's parents. The responsibility for the cost of the honeymoon generally falls to the bridegroom. It's not uncommon to see everyone but the bride's father having a whale of a time, while he surveys the scene with resignation and a bit of pleasure, pondering on the penury inflicted on him by a single night of revelry.

For young couples who don't have their parents consent, there is always Gretna Green. This nondescript Scottish town on the border with England is an odd choice for young couples from England to tie the knot. Under Scottish law, you do not need your parents' consent to get married past the age of 16, whereas in England, parental consent is required until you are 18. Commonly termed 'Scotland's Las Vegas', Gretna Green is the nearest town to the border with England and for years has been a Mecca for young English lovers dashing north across the border to get hitched on the sly.

Gretna Green has since lost some of its popularity, although the hotels there still bulge with red-sequined and heart-shaped four-poster beds to accommodate the romance of first love. The town itself is also famed for its nuclear submarines and is, in fact, a harsh environment for true romance to flower.

Saying Goodbye

I overheard two old ladies chatting about what they were up to that day in the queue for a bus one morning, "I'm going into town to do some shopping and then I'm off to the cremi in the afternoon," one of them explained. The 'cremi' was the local crematorium. The way the lady talked about going to see off a friend or loved one as though it was a trip to the hairdressers spoke volumes about the Scots attitude to death. There is no avoiding it so you may as well accept its inevitability with quiet resignation.

Funerals are held in churches or the chapels of crematoriums in Scotland, depending on how the dead prefer to be interred. Both follow a similar format. A short Christian service is given by the priest, including a summary of the life and achievements of the deceased. Hymns are sung and close family and friends stand up to give readings. Then the coffin is either carried outside by close family and buried in the graveyard, or wheeled into a flaming oven for cremation. If cremated, the family either buries or scatters the ashes at a scenic spot at a later date. The mood tends to be restrained and somber, outpourings of grief are generally reserved for more private moments.

Afterwards, a reception is held at a nearby hotel or family home. Do not be surprised if this can turn into a lively affair with a free flow of alcohol and conversation. Scots like to celebrate a life as much as mourn someone's passing and funerals are always a good chance to catch with more distant friends and relatives.

If you are invited to attend a funeral, it is best to dress in formal, dark clothes. Men tend to wear suits, women long dresses or a skirt and blouse. Turn up a good quarter of an hour before the service starts to avoid a very visible late entrance. If you want to give flowers, it is best to deliver them ahead time, rather than turn up clutching your floral tribute. At some point, you will be expected to give your condolences to the closest family of the deceased. This needs be no more than a handshake and an understanding nod of the head. If you are at any point in doubt about what you should be doing next, just keep quiet and follow the crowd.

HOMOSEXUALITY
Homosexuality is generally more accepted in Scotland than it used to be. Gay men and women can be more open about their sexuality now than even ten years ago, and there are well-established gay scenes in the big urban centres.

SETTLING IN

CHAPTER 5

'O ye'll tak' the high road, and I'll tak' the low road,
And I'll be in Scotland afore ye'
—'The Bonnie Banks of Loch Lomond',
a traditional song

VISAS AND WORK PERMITS
Nationals from the European Economic Area

Nationals from the European Economic Area (EEA) are entitled to visit, live or work in Great Britain. EEA countries are Austria, Belgium, Denmark, Finland, France, Germany, Greece, Iceland, Italy, Liechtenstein, Luxembourg, Netherlands, Norway, Portugal, Republic of Ireland, Spain and Sweden.

If you are a European Union (EU) national, you do not need to register with the police or get a residency permit. You only need to turn up with your passport, and if you intend to stay for longer than six months, prove that you are either working in the UK or have sufficient funds to support yourself. If you have family members who are not EEA nationals and who wish to come to the UK to live and work, they have to apply for an EEA family permit before they arrive.

After five years' residency in the UK, you can apply to stay indefinitely. To qualify, you have to have been working or financially self-supporting in the UK for at least four years and still have a right to residency. Applications take around 19 months to process.

Non-EEA Members

Citizens from European countries can visit Britain for up to three months with nothing more than a passport. US, Canadian, Australian and New Zealand citizens can stay for up to six months. Citizens from all other countries require a visa to visit the UK. Visitors can also choose to visit the UK on a business visa, provided they are employed overseas, conduct specific business activities and stay for no longer than six months.

Visitors who are not citizens of the European Union (EU) countries need a permit to work in the UK. In 2008 the visa application process was extensively overhauled. It is now impossible to get a work visa without the support of an established employer acing as an accredited sponsor. Visas are now determined on a points base system that takes into account factors such as qualifications, earnings and English language skills.

The popular Working Holiday Maker Entry Certificate for young people has been abolished and replaced by the Youth Mobility Scheme. This scheme allows nationals between 18 and 30 from Canada, New Zealand and Australia to work for up to two years.

Commonwealth citizens who were born before 1 January 1983 and have at least one parent who is a British citizen are considered British nationals. Commonwealth citizens with a British grandparent can also live and work in the UK for up to four years by claiming United Kingdom ancestry. If you are married to a British citizen, you can apply for British nationality provided it isn't a marriage of convenience for the sole purpose of gaining entry to the UK.

Students

Anyone can come to study in the UK provided they can prove that they are enrolled in a course of study involving a minimum of 15 hours organised daytime study per week. Prospective foreign students can also stay in the UK for up to six months, provided they can fund themselves as well as any course that they enrol in. Visa nationals still need to apply for a student or prospective student visa.

Foreign students are allowed to work for up to 20 hours a week part-time during term time but cannot take full-time vacancies. A foreign student's wife or husband and any children under 18 can join them. They are also entitled to work if the course of studies lasts for more than 12 months.

Application guidelines and the relevant documents are available on the joint Home Office and Foreign and Commonwealth Offices UK visas website:

http://www.ukvisas.gov.uk.

Asylum in the UK

Anyone who reaches the United Kingdom can claim asylum. The Home Office will then decide if they have a well-founded fear of persecution in the country that they are fleeing from.

During this time, asylum seekers are given accommodation and a voucher food allowance, instead of cash. The voucher system has come under much criticism as asylum seekers can only spend their money in shops that accept vouchers. Organisations that work with asylum seekers feel this is demeaning and that the system denigrates and stigmatises asylum seekers by making them feel they are separate from the rest of society.

There are no official figures on the number of refugees in Scotland but under the government policy of dispersing asylum seekers out of the London area, numbers are on the rise. The highest concentrations of refugees are in Glasgow.

A ROOF FOR THE NIGHT

Temporary accommodation is as varied as it is plentiful in Scotland. At the top of the range, there is the country's ubiquitous trademark, the historic castle. No longer damp and miserable sites of siege and starvation, many castles these days offer luxury accommodation for the few that can afford it.

If you find a castle is too ostentatious—or expensive—a good second option is an old shooting lodge. Many of these have been converted into hotels, giving a glance at a whole lifestyle as well as a warmish bed for the night. But lodges are often draughty and poorly heated, so bring plenty of warm clothing.

Hotels and inns are common across Scotland and serve a double function. They provide accommodation for tourists in the country at reasonable prices ranging from £ 20–£ 40 on average. They often also house the local bar for residents in the off season. So if you are looking for a slice of reality, check out the hotel bar, often tucked away from the rest of the hotel. The stained tartan carpet, scuffed up pool table and assortment of rough-looking characters around the bar can seem intimidating at first. But if you take the time for a few drinks, you'll have a great night and learn more about Scotland than you would from any number of guidebooks.

Next in line is the good old bed and breakfast, known as a B & B. These are a unique British institution and another good way of meeting locals while supporting the local economy. A bed and breakfast is a home that is owned privately and opened to travellers to stay in spare rooms. For as little as £ 20 a night per person, you can expect to get a comfortable room and feast on a legendary cooked breakfast in the morning.

You can't miss bed-and-breakfast establishments, drive into Fort William and there is a sign in front of every other house offering rooms, all in fierce competition with their neighbours. The only downside is that in a small house, you may feel like you are invading the family's personal space and end up tiptoeing around on eggshells, desperately trying to be invisible.

Youth hostels are traditionally the best budget option for putting a roof over your head for a night. Despite their name, they are open to anyone of any age, offering a bunk bed in a shared, single-sex dorm.

The Scottish Youth Hostelling Association (SYHA) is the biggest organisation that runs hostels. Their brochure, available in any tourist information office, details an impressive array of settings. Many of their hostels are old country houses set in beautiful countryside. Their flagship, Carbisdale Castle in Sutherland, has 197 beds and a collection of the finest privately owned Italian marble statues in Britain.

Sporting lodges are not for the fainthearted. Expect to dine surrounded by the stuffed animal trophies of wild beasts that made it to the dinner table. Most of these lodges offer fishing and shooting in as a package and are usually booked for weeks at a time by big groups during the summer.

The SYHA has gone a little more upmarket in recent years, and prices for a night are now comparable to bed-and-breakfasts (between £ 12 and £ 20). However, they do offer kitchen facilities, a television lounge, breakfast and plenty of information on various outdoor activities. Other independent youth hostels tend to be cheaper.

For many who visit Scotland, particularly the Highlands, comfort is an unwanted luxury. Hardened hillwalkers and climbers expect adversity, and sleeping on a roll mat on boggy ground somehow adds to the authenticity of the experience. Enter the camper's world, where there is no finer pleasure than a can of baked beans with cheese heated up on the primer gas stove after a long day's walk.

Campsites are plentiful, offering parking, showers and toilets for no more than a few pounds a night. Once in the Highlands, it is not always necessary to find a campsite. With ample free space to choose from, you can often pitch a tent anywhere as long as you are out of sight of the road and the local farmer. As long as you don't leave any litter or end up burning down the local woods, most locals will turn a blind eye.

A *bothy* is a good way station on a rain-blown evening with failing light, especially when you're faced with the prospect of spending a restless night under canvas. *Bothies* are unique public spaces that hold something of the open free spirit of the Highlands. No more that an empty cottage with a few beds and a stone hearth, they are open to anyone who happens to be passing and needs shelter. *Bothies* are free to stay in and rely on the good will of walkers to leave them tidy with the fire set and perhaps some spare food for the next travellers.

You can't get to a *bothy* by car; they are scattered across the most inhospitable areas of the Highlands and have undoubtedly saved countless people who would have otherwise perished in a sudden blizzard. Most *bothies* in Scotland have been meticulously marked on Ordnance Survey maps, so they shouldn't be too hard to find.

If all else fails, there is always a night under the stars, not as impossible a prospect as it may seem in Scotland. My most

The tatty visitor's books found in *bothies* tell countless tales of long walks and tall tales told round the fire in years past. One of the most chilling legends comes out of Barrisdale on the isolated Knoydart peninsula.

Legend has it that a giant pterodactyl-like flying beast frequents the valley and occasionally dines on passing travellers. On windy nights, there are numerous stories of the Barrisdale Beast descending onto the roof of the *bothy* in the valley, and clawing at it to get at the terrified walkers within.

memorable night in the great outdoors was spent in a sleeping bag on the shores of Loch Awe. A midnight sky cleared to put on a brilliant show of Northern lights. Sheets of shimmering colour and cartwheels of fairy lights lit up the lake in front. I fell asleep trying to imagine how people saw those lights before they were explained away by scientific reasoning; they must have seemed to be a message from somebody's gods. We woke the next morning to a grey leaden sky and frost on our sleeping bags. The magic had definitely moved on.

RENTED ACCOMMODATION

Rooms, flats and houses for let are advertised in local papers and most estate agents. It is also worthwhile going to the area that you would like to live in and looking at the notice boards of newsagents and cafés. This is the quickest and easiest way of finding rooms in shared flats or houses. Landlords may ask for bank and personal references before considering you as a tenant.

Once you have agreed to rent a place, you will be expected to pay the landlord or landlady the first month's rent in advance as well as a deposit. The deposit is generally two times the monthly rent, but this can vary. The deposit is returnable when you leave, provided that you have not damaged the property and are up to date with your rent. The landlord is responsible for repairing general wear and tear on a property, such as broken electrical appliances.

Unscrupulous landlords often withhold deposits on false pretexts, such as claiming that a tenant was responsible for damages made before they arrived. I have even heard of one case where the landlord claimed a tenant had stolen an entire sofa that was never there in the first place. Make sure your landlord gives you an inventory of the contents when you move in and check that everything on the list is there. It is also worth pointing out, or even photographing any existing damage, so that you aren't made to pay for it when you leave.

You will also have to sign a tenancy agreement with the landlord. Make sure that you read this carefully before you sign your life away; landlords can sneak in unreasonable demands. A standard tenancy agreement is for one year, but this sometimes includes a get-out clause for the tenant requiring a month's notice should you need to leave early.

Renting a place in Scotland can be expensive. There is the government's community charge tax to pay, which varies depending on the value of the property but runs into hundreds of pounds a year. Properties occupied by full-time students are not subject to community charge. However, if one or more of the occupants is not a student, the tax is levied regardless.

Water, electricity and gas bills are sent out quarterly. If you don't pay the first bill, you will be first sent a reminder and then finally a red reminder. This gives you seven days to pay up or face credit black listing, legal action and having your supply disconnected. Discounts are sometimes given if you pay your bills promptly. All televisions require television licences, an annual fee of around £ 150. If you don't pay your television licence, you may get fined £ 1,000.

Bills are most commonly paid by sending a cheque in the post. However, a more convenient method is direct debit, where an agreed amount of money is taken directly out of your bank account on a set date each month. Direct debit is now used to pay for everything from bills and rent to subscriptions, insurance and contact lenses.

BUYING YOUR OWN HOME

In Scotland, and Britain in general, there is a peculiar mythology that surrounds house ownership. Although most start out their independent lives in rented accommodation, most people aspire one day to actually have their own property. This is unlike other continental countries, such as

France, where it is normal to take on long term lets rather than actually buying a home.

The reasons are both social and financial. Buying a flat or a house is widely recognised as a prudent investment. After all, why give money away to a landlord when you can pay off a mortgage that will eventually give you your own house instead? Buying property is also considered a good bet because as the value of the house rises with time, so too does the equity in it. Although the housing market is prone to bust as well as boom cycles, property generally appreciates in value, and large profits can be made from buying and selling at the right moment.

Owning your own house is also an important step in life for those who can afford it. It is a measure of sound material progress, that one is moving on in life. In a nation of home lovers, your own flat or house becomes your castle of private seclusion and social respectability.

If someone in Scotland feels financially confident enough to take the plunge and buy a property, they embark on a complex road. The first step is to secure a mortgage from a bank or a building society, as few can afford to pay up front with their own capital.

Since the global credit crunch, lenders have tightened their lending criteria and mortgages have become a lot harder to come by. To have any chance of securing a mortgage, you need to be borrowing substantially less than the full purchase price and have an immaculate credit rating. The mortgage is then determined on the applicant's employment history and long-term job security.

Some companies also require life insurance to cover themselves in case you drop dead one day. One friend had problems getting life insurance for a mortgage because his medical records showed that he had smoked. You can also be discriminated against if you have been to the doctor for stress or emotional problems. So be wary, as any evidence that you are human or mortal may work against you!

There are a number of different types of mortgages and it is worth shopping around for the best deal. The simplest involve paying off the loan with a set interest in monthly

Many Scottish people aspire to own a home, whether it be a house with its own garden, or a small apartment in a block of flats.

instalments. An Australian mortgage works on the same principle, but calculates the interest daily on the money owed. In theory, this means paying less. An endowment mortgage is a form of insurance policy that invests the money you pay in. At the end of the term, you should get a lump sum that equals the amount of your mortgage and, in theory, make a profit as well. There have been problems with these in recent years, and it's worth taking financial advice before committing. Most mortgages are repaid over a 25-year period, although this is flexible.

Houses are advertised through property sections of newspapers, on the Internet, or by estate agents and solicitors. It's best to decide on the area you would like to live in, and then scout around the estate agents, solicitors and papers local to that area.

The *Solicitor's Property Guide* is a particularly good source as it pools 90 per cent of all properties for sale through solicitors across Scotland. The information is divided up into regions and is available in a weekly publication. The website http://www.espc.co.uk is fast becoming the first port of call if you are buying a home, as most estate agents now also advertise on the Internet. Some sites have as many as 75,000 properties for sale at one time, but if they aren't updated regularly, this can become frustrating.

The intrigue starts once you spot the property of your dreams. The seller will have set an asking price, which is usually below what they hope to get for it. Potential buyers then make bids for the house, often well over the asking price when the housing market is going well. Normally they add 10 per cent and then a few thousand on top for good measure. These offers are made independently through solicitors and there is no way of telling how much the others are bidding. After a set deadline has expired, the seller picks the highest offer and the deal is signed and sealed.

The advantage of this very Scottish system is that once the seller has agreed to a price—orally or formally on paper—they are legally committed. They are bound to sell to that person and can't get cold feet and pull out at the last moment without severe penalties. If you have had your bid accepted, this also means that someone else can't cut in with a higher price—known in the trade as *gazumping*—and snatch the place from under your nose.

This varies sharply with the system in England and Wales. It is filled with uncertainty for both the buyer and seller, an agreed offer that can be reneged on by both parties at any time. It's only when the legal contracts are signed and exchanged by both parties that the deal is set in stone. I have heard of countless horror stories of people who thought they had tied things up only to have the other party pull out hours before the formal papers were due to be signed.

After five years of meteoric price rises, the property market spectacularly collapsed in 2008 and 2009, with house prices plummeting by an average of 20 per cent across the UK. In Scotland, the market has fared a little better, with prices falling less dramatically in cities like Edinburgh and Aberdeen.

Sellers are now obliged to produce a Home Information Pack when they put a property on the open market. This report includes a survey for potential problems such as damp rot and subsidence, an assessment of the properties energy efficiency and a market valuation. The report is made available to all potential buyers and costs the seller anything between £ 400 and £ 1000

At the end of the day, the actual value of the property and the number of people interested may have no relation to how much the place is eventually sold for. Markets are vulnerable to many imponderables such as state of the economy, confidence and fashion. The simplest way of measuring the property market is to read property magazines and compare prices in the area you are interested for comparable properties. Estate agents will also tell you how much previous similar properties have been sold for.

It's worth noting that the cost of buying a house can far exceed what you pay the seller. The solicitor, essential for all the negotiations and legal transactions, will usually charge 1 per cent of the value of the property. However, this fee can go up if the value of the property is particularly high. Then there is the fee for the estate agent. There is also a 1 per cent government tax, called a stamp duty, that has to be paid when buying a house or flat.

TELEPHONES

Gone are the days when a whole community would be connected into one local operator. In the Sound of Sleat in the south of the Isle of Skye, one local resident told me how 60 years ago, she used to pick up the phone and talk directly to the operator, who would then put her through to the house she was calling. The only problem was that the whole community could quietly pick up their receivers and listen into the conversation. Everything said over the phone became public knowledge.

British Telecom (BT), then the state monopoly holder on telecommunications, has become considerably more sophisticated. Now an impressive array of cordless phones, fax phones, itemised bills, phone cards and answer services are on offer. Since becoming privatised, BT now has a whole field of competitors so do shop around. Some of these companies, such as Planet Talk, offer extremely cheap international rates. Mobile phones have become a must-have for old and young alike in the UK. There are a whole myriad of different options available, from simple 'pay as you go' phones to complex contracts with monthly payments.

INTERNET

The advent of broadband high speed Internet connection has revolutionised the use of the Internet. For a monthly fee, broadband gives constant Internet access at far greater speed than the old dialup method, without interfering with the phone line. Broadband is available from a number of different suppliers and a variety of different speeds and prices, so it is well worth shopping around before you jump on the super information highway.

With more secure means of shopping online, the Internet is now used as a gateway to a global supermarket with everything you could possibly imagine for sale at your fingertips. You can also book and pay for train journeys, flights, pay bills and even manage your own bank account online.

With most people in Scotland linked up to the Internet, Internet cafes are becoming scarcer and scarcer. However, a few have survived around train stations and in towns where lots of visitors who need to check their emails are passing through.

NUMBER CRUNCHING

Business numbers are advertised in the hefty *Yellow Pages*, delivered free to all. Private numbers and businesses are listed in local directories called *The Phone Book*. This blue book also includes information on dialling codes and the numbers of essential services. Dial 118-118 to talk to an operator who will look up numbers for you, provided you have the name of the business and town you are looking for. An international operator is available on 155. Calls made from phone boxes are currently free but cost around £ 0.50 each time from a domestic telephone.

Dial 999 to contact the emergency services—police, fire, ambulance and mountain rescue services. This number is for emergencies only. The Samaritans offer a 24-hour confidential emotional support for anyone in crisis—tel: (0345) 909-090. Scottish Women's Aid—tel: (0131) 475-2372—offers confidential help to women in crisis.

TRANSPORTATION
Airplanes
Most international flights fly into one of London's four airports: Gatwick, Heathrow, Luton or Stansted. The airline companies British Airways, Go, Air UK, Ryanair and Easy Jet offer the most frequent connections from London airports to either Glasgow's Preswick Airport or Edinburgh airport. Flights generally cost from £ 55 one way, but you can find deals for as little as £ 30 return. From Edinburgh and Glasgow, you can fly on to Aberdeen, Inverness or to another of Scotland's 17 internal airports. Internal flights are operated by British Airways Express.

There are several daily non-stop flights to Glasgow from New York, Chicago and Boston in North America. Fares vary depending on the time of year. The low season is from mid-January to the end of February and then October through to November. The high season is from mid-May until the end of August.

Ever since the Vikings first landed in Scotland, links have been retained with Norway by sea. In June and August, the Smyril line sails between Shetland, Norway, the Faeroe Islands, Iceland and Denmark. A more direct route is from Bergen in Norway to Lerwick in Shetland and then on to Aberdeen with P&O Ferries. The crossing has a reputation for being a rough one.

Many tourists coming from mainland Europe prefer to take shorter crossings to the North of England and then drive to Scotland. North Sea ferries sail from Rotterdam and Zeebrugge to Hull. From there, it's only a four-hour drive to Scotland. From Newcastle in the North of England, it is also possible to sail to and from Bergen and Stavanger in Norway, Gothenburg, Amsterdam or Hamburg. Further South, Stena Sealink and P&O Ferries offer frequent connections between Dover and French ports, but the drive north is considerably longer, taking up the best part of a day. To jump over to that other Celtic heartland, Ireland, there are two ferry services running from Scotland. P&O Ferries runs daily sailings from Stranraer to Belfast and European Ferries connects Larne with Cairnryan.

Trains

The guard at the tiny Highland station of Dalwhinnie swings his heavy green lantern and the old diesel train starts to pull away at a walking pace. It's night and the Isle of Iona sleeper from Inverness to London has a long, jolting way to go before it reaches the big city. It seems in no hurry, content to beetle on slowly south, a row of lights under a starless night.

Train travel holds a certain romance in Scotland. Locals and tourists alike are fond of routes like the overnight sleeper to Inverness or the stunning trip from Inverness to the Kyle of Lochalsh on the west coast.

The train network in Scotland is not as extensive as it was before many of the smaller branch lines were closed in the mid-sixties. Areas of Scotland such as the borders in the south and the far north-west coast are poorly connected.

The most popular routes are regular and efficient. For example, trains leave every 15 minutes between Edinburgh and Glasgow. With rail privatisation in the early nineties making the network profit-driven, routes to less popular destinations are being increasingly neglected and can often suffer delays.

Train information is available at the stations or on a central number—tel: (0345) 484-950. You can buy train tickets and reserve seats with cash or credit card either directly at the station, over the phone or online. As the network has been sold off to different private companies, you need to book over the phone from the company that operates the particular route that you are travelling on. The Great North Eastern Railway (GNER) travels between London, Edinburgh and Inverness. Virgin trains travel between London and Glasgow, and Scotrail covers most train travel within Scotland.

Trains are so popular to some enthusiasts that you may see small men with beards and notepads at some station platforms, eagerly writing down the names and registrations of passing trains. They are an exclusive breed known as trainspotters—as far as I know, they are peculiar to Britain.

Train fares in Scotland, and across Britain as a whole, tend to be expensive compared to other European countries. For example, a standard return from Edinburgh or Glasgow to London—four hours of travel each way—costs around £ 80. That is only for standard accommodation, first class costs over £ 100. Smoking is now prohibited on all trains.

It is possible to find cheaper fares. Travel on Fridays and peak holiday dates is always more expensive. There is the option of booking one week in advance for an Apex or two weeks in advance for a super Apex ticket. These fares give up to a third off on the standard ticket price. However, you have to commit yourself to your travel dates in advance and the ticket is non-refundable if you wish to travel at another time.

If you are under 26 or a full-time student, it is well worth buying a student railcard. This is a rail pass that gives one-third off all destinations. They cost £ 25 for a year and are available from any ticket office. You are required to show proof of age or that you are a full-time student if you ask for one. There is a similar card for families and those over 60 also offering up to one-third off rail travel. There are also central Scotland and Highland Rover tickets that offer deals for passengers who plan to tour around the country by train.

Buses and Post Vans

Bus travel is a considerably cheaper means for getting around Scotland, especially in the more isolated areas that can't be reached by train. A typical overnight return fare from London to Glasgow or Edinburgh is £ 30. Tickets and information are available directly from the bus stations.

National Express is the main operator between Scotland and England. The bus company Stagecoach also has extensive coverage within Scotland. Buses are considerably cheaper than train travel, but tend to be more cramped and uncomfortable. A student discount card as well as concessionary rates for children is available.

Numerous backpacker tours offer flying visits into the Highlands in a minibus with food, accommodation and a tour guide thrown in. Departing from Edinburgh or Glasgow, a typical three-day tour costs a very affordable £ 100. Running on very tight schedules, these tours can involve much more sitting in a crowded bus than actually exploring the Highlands.

In the Highlands, the smaller villages are most easily accessed by the post vans. These red station wagons or land rovers race from community to community, dropping off mail, messages and packages as they go. For a small fee, you can take a ride in the back of one of them, provided your destination is on their route. The post van times are available from local post offices, but you need to allow a good margin to pick one up either way. Due to the speed at which they negotiate the small winding roads, they are often ahead of time.

Ferry

Ferry travel is more than a quaint way to see Scotland; it is an essential means of transport to and from the 130 inhabited islands scattered around the coast. The company Caledonian Macbrayne runs most of the routes, all of them with roll-on roll-off car ferries. The main exceptions are the routes from Scrabster to Orkney and Aberdeen to the Shetland Isles, which are operated by P&O.

Ferry transport isn't cheap. The best option, if you plan to jump from island to island, is to buy an Island Hopscotch or Island Rover ticket, which offers multiple sailings over a set period of time at an economy price. It is advisable to reserve a place ahead of time during the peak period (April–

October) if you are taking a car. During the winter months, many run limited services and some non-essential routes dry up altogether.

Hitching

Scotland has a strong car culture and hitching isn't that common when most have their own transport. However, it is a common sight to see bedraggled walkers in the summer in the Highlands, desperately trying to hitch a ride with their mountainous backpacks filled with mouldy clothes.

To hitch a ride, find a suitable lay-by and stand looking mournful and harmless with your thumb up and the rest of your hand closed in a fist. It helps to write your destination on a big piece of card. Be prepared for a wait, there is little charity on the roads in Scotland. Hitch at your own risk—it is not safe for women to hitch alone.

AROUND TOWN

Taxis are plentiful in all of the main cities. The safest and most reliable are the black cabs, with their bright orange 'Taxi' sign on the front of the roof. When the light is switched off, it means the taxi is occupied.

Taxis are expensive. A short trip across town will start at an average of £ 6. Tipping is not necessary in Scotland but is always appreciated, especially if the driver takes the time to help you with you baggage. Buses are much cheaper (from £ 1 a ride), but their erratic frequency and speed and can be bewildering.

Glasgow has its very own Metro system, known as the underground. It is a modest affair compared to the jumble of lines that crisscross under London, but no less effective. For £ 1.20, you can travel the length of the city, from north to south and east to west.

The simplest way to get around is on foot. With the exception of Glasgow, which is too large to stroll around easily, cities in Scotland are small enough to explore on foot. A–Z maps found in most bookshops and newsagents make direction finding relatively easy and if you're lost, there is always a local to help you out. The Scottish love to give directions, occasionally walking with you some of the way to make sure you're on the right track.

DRIVING IN SCOTLAND

Britain drives on the left. That includes Scotland, Wales, Northern Ireland and England, so beware if you are used to driving on the right. It's easier not to get confused if you drive a British car with the steering wheel on the right-hand side.

There is a peculiar country code if you are driving in the Highlands. Much of this remote country is covered with single-track roads with passing places, meaning you can't pass an oncoming vehicle without one of you pulling over. It also makes overtaking impossible and long queues can form behind slow-moving cars and caravans. Passing places are also there for slow cars to pull in for cars behind to overtake. Pulling over to let people pass isn't a law but it is the custom, and if ignored can infuriate fast-moving locals who know the roads.

If someone pulls over to let you by, it is important to thank them either with a raised hand or a flash of your lights. If one hand is on the gear stick and the other on the wheel, just lift your index finger up off the wheel to signal your appreciation.

Car hire is relatively affordable in Scotland. You can hire a car for an average of £ 25 a day with nothing more than a valid UK or International driving licence and your credit card details. If you damage the hire car or van on your travels, you will be obliged by all hire companies to pay a part of the damages. This varies between £ 100 and £ 250; any more is covered by their insurance. The bigger companies such as Arnold Clark have centres across Scotland, so if you wish, you can pick up a car in Glasgow and drop it off in Inverness.

Driving Licence

You can get a British driving licence from the age of 17 by passing a driving test at a local test centre. Driving tests are notoriously rigorous in Britain and involve both a practical test of driving skills on the road and a written test of driving rules and regulations.

While learning to drive, you are allowed to brave the open road provided you have a provisional licence, are insured and have someone with a full licence in the passenger seat at all times. An 'L' plate must be attached to the front and back of the vehicle to show you are still learning to drive.

Beware of getting caught short without any petrol. In the Highlands, petrol stations can get pretty sparse. In the more isolated areas, some of the smaller pumps can also be closed on Sundays. There is nothing worse than spending an afternoon driving with your eyes fixed on the petrol gauge rather than the surrounding scenery.

Driving instructors offer courses of tuition running up to the test day for around £ 35 an hour. With the advent of the virtual world of computer technology, some driving tuition centres also offer virtual driving simulation for a fraction of the price of normal lessons.

By law, you are required to update the address on your driving licence if you move house. This is a simple affair that involves filling out part of the licence and sending it off to be changed. The process takes around ten days, during which time you can continue driving. If you are caught with an old address on your licence, you are liable for a heavy fine. Driving licences are valid right up until the age of 70, when it is required to have a sight test to keep driving on the road.

Buying into the Car Culture

Buying a car or motorbike anywhere in the world can be a risky business, especially if it's second-hand. Buying a car new from a showroom or second-hand from a dealer is relatively straightforward as they all come with a guarantee that covers hidden problems.

The riskiest but cheapest option is to buy directly from the last owner. Cars and motorbikes are advertised in a number of magazines, the biggest ones being *Auto Trader* and *Supermarket*. To avoid paying too much for a second-hand car, the magazine *Parker's Used Car Guide* gives an accurate and up-to-date guide on how much you can expect to pay for a particular model and age.

It is worth having a local mechanic look at a second-hand car before you commit. This can be arranged at a local garage for a fee, or the Automobile Association (AA) will send out one of their mechanics to have a look for around £ 160. Once you have bought a vehicle, it needs to be registered in your name. The previous owner will have the vehicle registration document, to which you add your details and send it off to the Vehicle Registration Centre in Swansea.

All vehicles need to have a valid road tax certificate. Road tax varies between £ 0 and £ 400, depending on the size and the level of carbon dioxide emissions of the engine. It is also possible to pay for road tax every six months. It is illegal to have a car on the road (even parked) with an out-of-date tax disk.

To buy a road tax certificate, you have to show a valid Ministry of Transport (MOT) certificate and insurance policy for the vehicle. The MOT test is carried out yearly on all vehicles by garages and MOT centres. The test is an evaluation of the general roadworthiness of the vehicle. If the vehicle fails on any count, relevant repairs need to be carried out before the certificate can be issued.

Insurance policies can be bought over the phone from any number of companies or brokers listed in the yellow pages. There are two types of policies. Third-party fire and theft will cover any damage to other vehicles if you are in an accident. It will also pay for the vehicle if it is stolen or suffers fire damage. Fully comprehensive, which is generally more expensive, also covers any damage to your own vehicle, including bumps or accidents which are your own fault. Insurance cover starts from around £ 300.

If you are involved in an accident with another vehicle, it is important to exchange vehicle licence plate numbers and names and addresses with the other driver. The details of payment for damages are then negotiated between each driver's insurance company. If you are in a crash and the other driver tries to make a getaway, make a note of their licence plate and the police can track them down.

It is worth becoming a member of a breakdown and recovery service in case you get stranded on a roadside. For a one-off payment of around £ 100 a year, you can call up for on-the-spot roadside repair or receive transport to the nearest

The Ross Fountain in Princes Street Gardens with Edinburgh Castle in the background. The park offers a lovely respite from the noise and bustle of the city.

A leisurely afternoon in the Grassmarket. One of the most vibrant areas in Edinburgh, the Grassmarket is a favourite with visitors and locals alike.

A view of the picturesque Loch Maree. Scotland's reputation for stunning landscapes is well deserved.

An exhibition at the McLellan Gallery.

Dancers at the Braemar Gathering and Highland Games. A much loved summer event, the Highland Games are an enjoyable, authentic Scottish experience.

garage if the problem can't be patched up there and then. The biggest companies with nationwide coverage are the RAC (tel: 0800-887-766) and the AA (tel: 0800-828-282).

THE COLOUR OF MONEY

Anyone can open a bank account in Britain provided they can show proof of identity and proof of address. Proof of identity can be a passport, driving licence, photo identity card, pension or benefit book or birth certificate. Proof of address can be a current household bill (gas, electricity, telephone, water and council tax) or another official document which shows your name and address, such as a bank or credit card statement.

Banks, building societies and the post office offer a wide range of different types of accounts with varying degrees of interest, so it is well worth looking around before committing. Most banks also offer credit cards.

With the introduction of direct banking in Britain, it is becoming easier to manage an account. You can now make a phone call or log onto the Internet to pay bills, check balances and order cheque books. Although this is all very neat, it does threaten thousands of branch office jobs, which may no longer be needed to help deal with customer accounts and inquiries.

Cash machines are the most common way to withdraw money in Scotland. Most banks and building societies have cash dispensing machines outside their offices. Cash machines are well networked and it is possible to take out money and check your account from most bank and building society machines, regardless of whether or not you bank with them. Some cash tellers will charge up to £ 2 a transaction for this service.

While most currencies in Europe are now standardised under the euro, Britain is still reluctant to join. The pound sterling currency—divided into 100 pence—is the same in Northern Ireland, Wales, England and Scotland, although the designs on the coins and notes can differ.

Coins are straightforward, as the distinctive sizes for differing denominations don't vary. There are £ 2 and

£ 1 coins and then 50 p, 20 p, 10 p, 5 p, 2 p and 1 p coins. Scottish notes printed by the Royal Bank of Scotland, the Bank of Scotland and the Clydesdale bank are very distinctive, proudly sporting the heads of famous entrepreneurial Scottish figures. Notes printed from the Bank of England, Scotland or Northern Ireland are also legal tender throughout the British Isles.

POST

The Royal Mail, one of the few remaining public services in Britain, is fast and efficient. Mail is delivered to the door, seldom lost and is easy to post from the multitude of little red boxes that have become something of a trademark for the British Isles. When addressing mail, it's important to follow a clear order:

- Addressee's name
- Building number or name
- Street name (if there is one)
- Locality name (if there is one)
- Post town (in capital letters)
- Postcode (in capital letters)

The postcode should always be on a separate line at the end of the address. If you don't know the postcode, call the enquiry line on tel: (08457) 111-222 or visit Postcodes Online at website: http://www.royalmail.co.uk. It is also recommended to put the return address on the back of mail; if it can't be delivered, Royal Mail will return it for free.

Stamps are bought in booklet in most newsagents or individually from post offices. First-class stamps cost 39 p for a letter under 60 grams and generally reach their destination the next day anywhere in the British Isles. A second-class stamp for a postcard or letter costs 30 p and takes around three working days to arrive. Heavier letters and packages cost more depending on their weight.

For an additional fee starting at £ 4.95. mail is guaranteed to be delivered the next day, provided it is sent before noon. To check that a recorded item has arrived, call tel: (08459) 272-100 or go to the Royal Mail's website at http://www. royalmail.co.uk.

Letters up to 20 g and postcards to the whole of Europe cost 48 p. Mail sent abroad can be sent by surface mail or, for a little more money but quicker delivery time, by airmail. All mail sent by air needs an airmail sticker, or 'PAR AVION—BY AIRMAIL', written on the top left hand corner of the letter or package. British Mail aims to deliver letters to Western Europe in two days following the day of posting and to countries outside of Europe in 4 days. Most packages containing goods that are sent outside of the EU need a customs label, available from post offices.

If you do not wish to have mail delivered directly to your home, you can arrange to have a PO Box set up. This is an alternative address where post is held until you pick it up at your local post office [to apply, call tel: (08457) 950-950]. If you move, you can also arrange to have mail sent on to a new address in the UK, or sent abroad via airmail, for up to two years.

CRIME

Scotland is a relatively law abiding and peaceful place. Although there is a rise in gangland style shootings in urban areas across Britain, the country does not have a gun culture and the police still walk the streets with little more than a baton and handcuffs. Stabproof vests and a chemical spray to ward off aggressors are to be introduced as standard for the police force, but the days of seeing coppers or bobbies on the streets with sidearms is still a long way off.

Simple precautions are the best way to ward off petty crime in Scotland. Lock up your vehicle, room or house when you leave it and don't leave valuable possessions in the car unattended. Avoid dark and unlit places in urban areas at night and be aware of who is around you when you take money out of a cash machine at somewhere quiet. If someone threatens you for money, give it to them; they aren't joking.

Tune into most Scottish news outlets on any given day and you will probably be chilled to the bone by breaking news of some grisly crime involving knives, drugs, sex or missing body parts. Don't worry, this is only the media's macabre interest in violent crime. Despite the impression given by all the over-zealous reporting, more serious crimes such as rape, assault or murder are in fact rare in Scotland. Most of the violence is domestic, or fights between young men—and occasionally women—late at night with a few drinks inside them. Like anywhere else in the world, women should take care if they are on their own in a town or city late at night. The further north you go into the Scottish Highlands, the safer it gets.

If you have been the victim of violence, call the police immediately on free phone 999 to report it. Officers will be sent out to investigate and there is more of a chance of catching the perpetrators than by finding a police station to report it. All other inquiries should be made at police stations.

THE WELFARE STATE

The welfare state, set up under the Liberal Prime Minister Lloyd George at the beginning of the last century aimed to provide state support for its citizens from the cradle to the grave. Over 60 years on, the welfare state is still in place. For all the system's bureaucracy and funding shortages—and there is plenty of both—it still provides a vital service to those who need it.

Health care is largely free for everyone and additional support is available for people who are struggling to keep their heads above water financially. This includes everyone from the unemployed to disabled people, pensioners, families and children. Help can come in many forms including cash payments, tax credit, housing, home help for the elderly and legal aid.

Health care and other state benefits, also known as social security, are available to anyone who is from a member country of the European Union (EU). Some countries outside of the EU also have reciprocal agreements with the UK. For example, Iceland, Liechtenstein and Norway are considered members of the EU when it comes to cash benefits.

People outside the EU are also eligible for social security if they are a refugee or a dependant of the widow or widower of anyone who was eligible. You cannot claim benefits if you are a full-time student. For specific information on benefits and related health care cover, contact:

Benefits Agency
Department of Social Security
Pensions and Overseas Benefit
Directorate
Newcastle on Tyne
NE98 1BA
Tel: (0191) 218-7777
Fax: (0191) 218-7293

Health Care

Health care under the National Health Service (NHS) is free for anyone who is eligible. The first port of call is the local doctor or general practitioner (known as a GP). To be assigned a doctor, you need to register with a health centre or doctor's surgery in the area. You only need to show that your permanent address is within that health centre's boundaries.

An appointment will then be made for you to have a general check up with your GP, after which you can make an appointment with him or her whenever you wish. After you have been registered, you can visit any health centre in the country for a temporary visit if needed. Visiting a doctor is free but prescriptions have to be bought and paid for at a pharmacy. If an ailment or injury needs further attention, a doctor will refer you to the appropriate specialist or hospital.

Health centres have emergency doctors available 24 hours a day for urgent cases. Most hospitals have an accident and emergency department that anyone can visit without an appointment if they need urgent treatment.

There is also a burgeoning interest in alternative medicines in recent years. It is now possible to find treatments such as acupuncture, homoeopathy, herbal medicine and osteopathy across Scotland. Most of these treatments are not funded by the NHS and must be paid for. Although a few GPs are willing to recommend these treatments to patients, they are unable to make a formal referral to anyone who isn't also a registered medical doctor.

Free dental care is also available to unemployed people on benefits. However, it is increasingly difficult to find dental practices that offer these services as many of them have become privatised.

Private Health Insurance

In recent years, the burden of an increasingly ageing population, together with funding problems, has put the NHS system under severe strain. As a result, some patients are having to go on long waiting lists for treatments. In response to this, a number of private health care companies have set up in the UK offering prompt care at a price. The two most popular companies that offer private health insurance are PPP International and BUPA International. The cost of this cover varies massively depending on your age and current health.

Other State Benefits

To claim state benefits, you need a National Insurance number. If you do not already have one, make an appointment at the local social security office. You need to bring proof of identity, such as a passport or driving licence. National insurance numbers take between three and six weeks to be assigned. During this time, any claims can be backdated but no benefits payment will be made until the National Insurance number comes through.

You may also have to take a habitual residency test to establish that you are living long-term in the country. This is largely to prevent foreign students from coming over to Britain and claiming benefit for a few months in the summer.

Job centres, scattered across the country, process claims and advertise work. There is a vast array of benefits forms on offer and claims are processed depending on individual circumstances.

The most common benefit is the job seekers' allowance, a weekly allowance of £ 55 a week to support people who are unemployed and looking for work. To qualify, you have to be available for work at any time and be willing to work part- or full-time.

People unemployed for the longer term, (six months or more for young people between the ages of 18 and 24 and over two years for those aged 25 or over), come under the 'New Deal'. Introduced under the Prime Minister Tony Blair in 1998, the 'New Deal' offers support with education and training, as well as greater pressure to find work.

If you are unemployed, or earn less than £ 60 a week, you can also claim housing benefit. Housing benefit will pay the rent for you. There is currently a three- to six-month backlog on claims. Although the rent money is backdated to when you first made a claim, many landlords prefer not to wait and will not accept tenants who wish to claim housing benefit.

ENTERTAINMENT FOR CHILDREN

There is no single system in Scotland for the care of small children. Daycare for children under the age of three is available at private, community run or workplace nurseries. The average cost for a place at a private nursery is £ 136 a week. Nursery places are provided by the Education Department for children aged three or over.

Another good form of daycare for small children is childminders. Childminders offer a secure environment for groups of children to play at their own home. Charges vary widely but expect to pay at least £ 3.50 an hour. All proper childminders have been registered and checked out by the Care Commission before they are allowed to offer this service.

In most areas, additional support is available from pre-school play groups. Organised and coordinated by the Scottish Pre-school Play Group Association, parents take turns to look after each other's children.

There are a huge variety of different activities available for older children. They include museums, galleries, castles, ghost tours, outdoors pursuits centers, wildlife reserves, amusement arcades and sports clubs. The best way of finding what is available near you is to ask a family that lives in the area, or check out the advertisements and listings in the local paper.

EDUCATION

Children start formal education at the age of four or five at primary school. Primary school runs for seven years until they reach high school. At high school level, those parents who can afford it will decide whether or not to send their children to state school, or to have them educated privately.

Private schools, often confusingly called public schools, offer more intensive tuition, better facilities and can be mixed or single sex. Private boarding schools take children off parent's hands completely during term time, providing accommodation and full catering on site. Gordonstoun, situated near Elgin in the Highlands, is a favoured choice for the Royals: Prince Charles and his father both studied there. Boarding schools are also famed for their obsession with punishing sports such as rugby and endemic bullying between students (euphemistically called *fagging*). All state schools are day schools.

School qualifications are the same regardless of what school you send your children to. After four years of high school or secondary school, students, usually when they are 15 or 16 years old, sit for their standard grade exams (usually seven exams). After this, they are free to leave, or they can study for one more year and sit for an average of five Highers. Entrance into higher education is dependent on exam results from the Highers.

The Scottish system differs from the English high school exams, which starts with GCSE's at standard grade levels and ends with the Highers equivalent of GCE Advanced levels. Advanced levels, also known as A levels, last two years rather than one and take on fewer subjects (usually three) in greater depth. A few of the privately run schools in Scotland offer the English system. Confusing as all of this sounds, it makes no substantive difference when it comes to higher education. Institutes of higher education within Great Britain and abroad accept both qualifications.

Around 50 per cent of the 60,000 school leavers in Scotland go on to some form of further education. There is no shortage of choice; there are 23 higher education institutes in Scotland. Fourteen of these institutes are universities (including the Open University) and the remainder are technical colleges which offer a wide variety of vocational courses and training.

There is more to offer in the fee-paying world than traditional public schools, or schools such as Gordonstoun. Rudolf Steiner's educational system was founded in 1919 to encourage children's personal development rather than pushing them through a rigid education system.

University degree courses last a year longer in Scotland than in England—four years on average rather than three. Students can choose to finish after three years if they wish, and be awarded a general degree. If they go the full course, they come out with a Masters with Honours. More than 38,000 students graduate every year from university.

The Scottish education system is highly valued both within Britain and abroad, drawing many foreign students to its shores. Many are attracted by the prestige of particular university faculties. For example, Herriot Watt has been famed for centuries for its excellence in medicine. So keen was the demand for bodies for autopsies and medical research in the 19th century that graves were frequently robbed in Edinburgh to keep up the supply. The gruesome tale of William Burke and William Hare's search for fresh specimens comes straight out of the darker days of scientific inquiry in Edinburgh.

The Two Williams

William Burke and William Hare are the world's most notorious body-snatchers. Over a 12-month period from 1827–1828, they murdered over a dozen people in Edinburgh and sold their corpses to a local anatomy school desperate for fresh bodies to dissect. When they were finally tracked down and caught by the police, Hare famously gave evidence against Burke in exchange for his own freedom. Burke swung from the gallows and Hare disappeared, never to be seen again.

Strathclyde University has one of the largest engineering facilities in the UK, with around 3,000 full-time students. The arts are also well represented. Glasgow University is famed for its art courses as well as the stunning building designed by Charles Mackintosh that houses them. The art department at Dundee University is also highly regarded.

These are just a few of the many examples of fine Scottish universities. Rebecca Castro from Chile who has just finished a Masters Degree in Computer Science from Napier University hopes to find a good job in the computer industry in the next few months. "The tuition is excellent and I'm confident that I can find work here or abroad with little problem," she told me. Mind you, with university courses costing foreign students anything from £ 7,000 a year for tuition alone, the standard of education needs to be pretty high.

Unlike many countries, most students study away from home after they have finished high school. Universities often offer shared accommodation in halls of residence for the first year or for postgraduate students, but most opt for shared squalor in a cheap flat.

This tradition is now changing. British university students used to be well looked after with state grants and free tuition. But students have struggled financially ever since the grants system was replaced by long-term loans and tuition fees. Although Scottish students do not have to pay tuition fees in Scotland, all UK students south of the border have to stump up around £ 2000 for every year of study. Fees for international students are scaled up to around £ 7,000 per annum.

As a result, many students are opting to study from home to keep costs down. Perhaps the new University of the Highlands and Islands (UHI), which aims to link students studying from home with different educational institutions via the Internet, is the sign of things to come.

SHOPPING

Shops have largely replaced markets in Scotland, with American-style malls increasingly becoming the norm in the cities. There are exceptions, most famously the Barras and Paddy markets in Glasgow, where you can pick up any hand-me-down or electrical goods of unknown origins for a fraction of the retail price.

Little goes to waste in Scotland. Charity shops recycle clothes, books and other bits and pieces to raise funds for the needy. Oxfam shops are the most famous, but there are plenty of other charity shops that sell stuff that would normally be thrown away. They are a good source of cheap shirts and the occasional bargain, sold at 1940s prices.

Second-hand bookstores are also a great source of pleasure to readers in Scotland. Tucked away in odd corners of towns and cities, they offer hours of dusty browsing in dimly lit labyrinths of shelves and boxes. There are some real gems: for example, the tiny bookstore in the village of Blair Atholl holds an impressive array of literature on Scottish myth, legend and folklore.

There are also plenty of junk shops that sell everything from old radios, bags, door handles and stuffed animals to the occasional genuine antique. Good deals can be sought privately in the 'for sale' sections of local papers or in car boot sales. A car boot sale is just that, a field where anyone can turn up and sell off their possessions from the boot of their car.

Bargaining or haggling is not the custom in Scotland, or in Britain in general. If something has a price tag on it, that is the price and you are expected to pay it without question. The only exceptions are if you buy something in bulk or offer to pay in cash, in which case it is occasionally possible to arrange some form of discount. It is perfectly acceptable, in fact expected, to drop the price a little in a market, but never more than 20 per cent of the value that's been quoted. The most you can say when hoping to get a price dropped is, "Is this your best price?"

Goods can be bought with cash, cheque or credit card. Shops and restaurants accept most credit cards. Clothing measurements are now standardised with the rest of Europe and are in metric.

FOOD AND ENTERTAINING

CHAPTER 6

'Scots whisky is just about the only thing left that brings
guaranteed and sustained comfort to mankind.'
—Lord Boothby, Member of Parliament, in 1984

MEALS

The British Isles are not known for gourmet cuisine. In fact, the standard fare is so unremarkable that rather than live on an eternal diet of 'meat and two veg', the British have virtually adopted international cuisine as their own.

Scotland is famed for fresh and wild produce such as salmon, venison and berries. But the harsh climate has traditionally restricted produce to a few staples. Root crops such as potatoes, carrots and swede have been plentiful since they were introduced in the 18th century, but fruit and vegetables more sensitive to the cold are largely imported from warmer climes.

In the past Scots have tended to rely on energy-rich carbohydrates to combat the cold, and who can blame them? With the wind whipping up a fury outside and icicles forming inside the kitchen, you can hardly imagine sitting down to a slice of melon, followed by an asparagus salad. The Scottish prefer to tuck into wonders such as a fish supper (cod and chips), mince meat and potatoes (*tatties* 'n' mince), blood sausage (known as black pudding), kippers and the king of them all—the mighty *haggis*.

Breakfast

The Scots don't shirk breakfast. The whole country tends to eat gargantuan breakfasts compared to much of continental Europe. The French or Italians settle for a coffee and a croissant in the mornings. Scotland is fuelled on bacon rolls, and that's just for starters.

The most traditional of breakfasts is, of course, porridge. This gloppy mixture of oats and water or milk can be delicious and sustaining. However, if badly prepared, it sticks to your gums, and when uneaten turns as hard as concrete.

Porridge was a staple diet to generations of Scots. Traditionalists of the older generation will swear that the only way to eat it is just with water and a dash of salt. My father told me that it was standard practice for men going out 'on the hill' to take a block of porridge that had been cooked until very thick, poured into a drawer and allowed to harden. It was then cut into slices and was the main food for the day.

These days, eating porridge doesn't have to be such an earnest affair; in fact, it can be very tasty indeed. Pinhead oatmeal, instead of rolled oats, soaked overnight and heated gently in a low oven is delicious. It is best mixed with anything from butter, cane sugar, cream, toasted almonds and fruit compote to maple syrup or even whisky to give it a hint of the exotic.

For many, a bowl of porridge is merely preliminary to the main act—cue drums and the sound of sizzling fat— the cooked breakfast. People visiting the British Isles are generally astounded by their first encounter with a cooked breakfast, also known as an English or Scots breakfast. Certainly, working through the mix of eggs, sausage, bacon, chips, mushrooms, toast, fried tomatoes, fried toast and tea demands both perseverance and courage. The Scottish version throws in a *tattie* scone, *haggis* and black pudding for good measure.

The *tattie* scone is a quintessentially Scottish invention, made all the more unusual by the fact that it looks more like a pancake than a scone. A good indication of the Scottish cuisine's traditional abhorrence of all things healthy can be found on the suggested meals on the back of one scone pack: 'Top with baked beans or cheese or cover with scrambled eggs and bacon.' Stodginess rules!

Cooked breakfasts are most commonly found in small cafés, often called 'greasy spoons'. Usually workman's cafés, these scruffy no-fuss institutions pour out an endless stream of fried food and gallons of stewed tea. The pictures on their walls of faded pastoral scenes contrast with the harsh scrape of stainless steel cutlery on china and the low drone of conversation. There is something both comforting and vaguely depressing about these places where time stands still, and few bother to take off their coats.

The more upmarket eateries offer more refined fare such as smoked salmon or herring (known as a kipper). This tastes best when grilled or poached in milk and eaten with a fried egg. Smoked herring, most famously made in Arbroath and known as 'Arbroath smokies', are a delicious throwback to Scotland's seafaring heyday.

Lunch

This can be a meagre affair if you're already carrying around the best part of Noah's Ark in your stomach. Lunches, particularly in cities and towns, tend to be taken quickly or on the hop. The exception is Sunday lunch, when many families sit down for a roast, usually lamb or beef, two boiled vegetables and roast potatoes with gravy.

Walking past a High Street baker between 12:00 pm and 2:00 pm will give you some idea of the typical Scottish lunchtime diet. School children and adults queue onto the streets for their rolls, pies, pasties, crisps and donuts. Scotland has a very sweet tooth. Sweets and chocolates are consumed non-stop by children. Every newsagent, general store and gas station has them laid out in racks like glittering jewels. My dentist once told me that she has to frequently fill holes in children's first set of teeth, let alone the second lot.

Tea

Tea at 11:00 am, known as elevenses, mid-afternoon tea at 4:00 pm and high tea at 6:00 pm are now a fading tradition. The demands of living and working in a modern world have largely put paid to these quiet moments in urban centres. In the country and in particular among the older generation however, teatime still holds sway as a daily ritual in the home.

Life and Tea

There is nothing more comforting than sitting with friends or family around a table carefully laid out with pots of tea and a collection of cakes and scones. My great-aunt Kat was a master at the British variation on the tea ceremony. Now in her nineties, she wouldn't entertain any help, chatting away as she busied herself with pots of tea and scones pulled straight from the oven to be smothered with butter, homemade jam and heather honey.

She would sit me down and pour the tea from a huge pot with her ancient hands. She was so petite that the teapot seemed to dwarf her and she practically used her whole body weight to counter lever the pouring tea.

Scones—plain or with cheese or raisins—are only a part of the traditional spread. There is also shortbread, oatcakes and Scottish pancakes. The pancakes are laden with butter and jam or honey. Cakes come in all shapes and sizes, but is generally make with dried fruit. The best known is the Dundee cake, a sweet malty loaf crammed with fruits.

In recent years, the importance of tea as a national cure-all waned a little with the arrival of good coffee. Up until recently, the only coffee you could find outside of home was ropy old filtered coffee in a teacup. Nowadays, you can find a decent cappuccino in most cafés. Café culture in the cities has taken over from the more formalised tradition of afternoon and high tea.

But a nice cup of tea—generally milky and without sugar—still holds a certain mystique in Scotland and Britain in general. It oils the wheels of social interactions and work breaks and provides comfort in times of crisis. It even defines you to some extent; the working classes go for the strongest blends with lots of tannin and sugar, middle-class folk drink the exotic and aromatic varieties such as Lapsang Souchong and Earl Grey and alternative types settle for herbal teas made from roots, flowers and bark.

Dinner

Dinner, also known as supper or sometimes as tea, is the most important meal of the day. It is generally served between 6:30 pm and 8:00 pm, remarkably early compared to Italian or Spanish standards. It's the great coming together of families, lovers and friends, when differences are laid aside or lain open again around the table.

What is on the table varies immensely, but Scotland offers an impressive array of native game and fish to choose from. Most famous is venison, or deer. Available all year round at no small expense, venison has a strong, distinctive flavour and is best roasted slowly with fresh berries such as juniper and blaeberries—also wild and native to the area. It is also wonderful in a casserole with a lot of red wine added to the pot.

There's plenty more wild game to choose from, such as hare, rabbit, partridge, pheasant, grouse, duck and pigeon. Wild game is tougher than the average chicken or lamb and is best marinated and cooked slowly. These days, game is rarely seen on the table. High prices, conservation concerns and the takeover of supermarket shopping have made such food increasingly the domain of exclusive restaurants.

Not so for the fruits of the sea. Being a part of the British Isles and surrounded by so many deep oceans, fish still makes up an important part of the diet. A good fishmonger in Scotland bristles with choice: oyster, muscle, crab, squat lobster, prawn, whitefish, herring, cod, flatties, monkfish, halibut, skate, mackerel and John Dory stare out from plastic trays at passers-by.

Most traditional of all is the herring. The herring once sustained thousands of fishermen up and down the coastlines. It's said that long before the toll bridge was built over to the island of Skye, you could walk over from the mainland hopping from small fishing boat to boat.

Herring was also a staple food for poor folk, smoked, salted or pickled to keep it longer. Salted herring would be soaked overnight, hung and grilled to make Buft herring or 'bufters', the 19th century version of deep fried cod. A classic Scots folk song praises the strength and bravery of Scots men before coming up with the explanation: 'For the lads have been fed upon tatties and herring'. Herring catches have long since been exhausted and even cod, the modern-day alternative, is becoming increasingly expensive as numbers dwindle.

Although fantastically fresh seafood, not to mention trout and salmon from the rivers, is still readily available in Scotland, the Scots aren't very inventive when it comes to preparation. Everything is generally fried in batter or grilled with butter and lemon. Fresh fish prepared simply is often the best: A small 'breakfast' trout—caught the same morning—rolled in oats and fried with butter settles any debate.

Tastes and culinary practices are also changing. Seafood cafés and restaurants now produce well-thought-out and carefully prepared dishes. The best plate of mussels I've had in my life, cooked with herbs and white wine, was in a tiny café on the island of Mull.

HAGGIS'N CLAPSHOT

Haggis with *tatties* and *neeps* come closest to being Scotland's national dish. It's certainly the first thing that comes to mind when one thinks of Scottish food, although this could have something to do with the memory of how long it lingered in the stomach the last time it was eaten. Dreamt up in a distant past when times were hard and livestock eaten down to the very marrow in their bones, the *haggis* is a creative way of using up what's left when the prime cuts are finished.

In short, it is offal, heavily disguised with oats, spices and pepper, but still offal. What it lacks in content, it doesn't exactly make up for in presentation either. The whole meal is blended and stuffed into a sheep's stomach to be baked or boiled and served up with more boiled *tatties* and *neeps*. You have to hand it to the Scots for coming up with the concept of the *haggis* as a national dish.

As awful as it all sounds, a *haggis* is surprisingly tasty on a chilly night with a tot of whisky over it. Another way to eat it is to slice it and fry it in butter until crisp.

One thing to look out for if you're a newcomer to Scotland is the standard joke about where 'the wild hairy *haggis*' is from. Reader beware! *Haggises* are not elusive Highland animals that live in the hills and have to be hunted and skinned for the table. Given half a chance, many Scots will reel out a complex description of the *haggis*' feeding habits and mating patterns before letting the perplexed visitor in on the joke.

The modern day *haggis* has been forced to accommodate a growing population of vegetarians in Scotland. Vegetarian or 'white *haggis*' is now a widely popular alternative to the old blood and guts version. However, the thought of introducing vegetables to the *haggis* concept, let alone excluding meat all together, is still unacceptable to some old traditionalists. One friend, Marcus Noble, took a white *haggis* back to his grandfather one Sunday, only to be virtually thrown out of the house along with the vegetarian offering. "Vegetarian *haggis*. How could you go that way?" his grandfather bellowed.

THE GRAVY TRAIN

A nice plump *haggis* is more a symbol of a uniquely Scottish food invention than something that is eaten daily by the population. These days, the Scots go for more generically British fare when it comes to the national pastime of eating heavy foods.

Chips, thick-cut and greasy, are a standard complement to a few beers. Bought from a late night *chippie* or chip shop, customers order their chips and choose a fish or meat product from a selection of objects laid out behind a brightly-lit glass-fronted counter. Their choice, generally a slice of cod or sausage, is dipped in a mixture of flour and water and then deep-fried in oil. The whole lot, chips and all, are wrapped in paper to be wolfed down with fingers on the street.

The Scots, creative in all aspects of life, have added to the usually limited chip-shop fare in their own inimitable style. There is the Scotch pie, bits of generic meat in gravy encased with crusty pastry, or the macaroni cheese pie for vegetarians. You can also wash down a few beers with a mini *haggis* deep-fried in batter or an obscenely large pink sausage.

Two Glaswegian inventions, deep-fried battered pizza and—wait for it—a battered chocolate or 'Mars' bar have been all the rage in the last few years. The 'Mars' bar is a little harder to find these days in an average *chippie*, but can be made up on the pleading request that you've never tried it before. Friends that have tried it have told me that it may wreck your waistline but is a small price to pay for a little slice of heaven.

After making a soggy selection from a Scottish *chippie*, you may be asked, "Salt 'n sauce?" (Most common in Edinburgh). This means: "Do you want salt and a thick brown liquid with a burnt barbecue taste over your greasy chips?" The man or woman behind that high *chippie* counter may as well be asking, "Would you like a premature heart attack from cholesterol overdose with your meal?" It's no wonder that Glasgow, the home of the battered pizza, also has the highest rates of heart disease in the Western world.

DOUGHNUT HEAVEN

Glasgow is no exception when it comes to diet-related illnesses in Scotland. Stodgy food and lack of exercise puts Britain at the top of the coronary heart disease table in Europe. According to the British Heart foundation, amongst European Community countries, only Ireland and Finland have a higher rate of heart attacks than Britain.

Ask any doctor in Scotland and they will tell you that the young don't eat enough fruit and vegetables and they drink and smoke too much when adults. The diets of the elderly aren't much better either.

I remember coming across a nurse who was cleaning out an old pensioner's house who had died the week before. She was pushing a wheelbarrow piled high with cans of tinned rice pudding, half of them long out of date. Apparently that's all he ate.

Neil Poulter, an eminent professor of preventative cardiovascular medicine at the Imperial College London, summed up the nation's predicament in the *Guardian* newspaper:

'We've got high levels of smoking, we've got a high fat intake, cholesterol levels are up and we're overweight. We've got high blood pressure and we have too much salt in our diet. And we don't exercise. More than 30 per cent of the population do nothing whatsoever apart from breathing. And it's getting worse.'

There is a growing shift in awareness of the importance of healthy eating amongst those who can afford it. Organic foods, produced without any pesticides or artificial fertilisers, are increasingly popular. In recent years there has also been a move towards more local food production, with farmers market springing up in many areas.

PUDDING

No proper sit-down meal in Scotland is complete without a sweet pudding.

What desserts in Scotland may lack in finesse, they more than make up for by being rich, yummy and filling. Nothing comes close to the taste of a good crumble, usually eaten hot and topped with cream, ice cream or custard. A crumble is made from whichever fresh fruit is in season, such as rhubarb, apple, gooseberry or damson, and then oven-baked with a crispy flour and butter topping.

There are plenty more sweet winter warmers that deserve a mention, but in the end, words alone won't do them justice. It's best if you can sample the taste of bread pudding or a jam roly-poly yourself. One old favourite is easy to make whether you're in Scotland or abroad. It is a Highland dish called *cranachan*, also called *cream crowdie*, served on special occasions. Note that my recipe calls for heather honey. Although this is not an essential ingredient, it tastes superb regardless of what it's poured into or spread onto.

Recipe for Cranachan Dessert

Ingredients

Double cream	0.3 litres/0.3 quarts
Toasted oatmeal	4 tablespoons (tbsp)
Whisky or Drambuie	3 tbsp
Heather honey	3 tbsp

Toast the oatmeal in the oven until crisp and lightly browned. Sweeten the cream to taste with heather honey. Whip the cream and whisky until it is thick, then fold the oatmeal into the cream and serve cool but not chilly.

What relatively limited fresh native fruits there are in Scotland are made good use of. Autumn in the Highlands is a time to fill the larder with an impressive array of jams, pickles and chutneys to preserve a taste of summer's fruits long into winter. I remember being sent out in September as a child with friends to pick blackberries or blueberries, only to come back with black mouths smeared with dark juice and a meagre half tub of fruit for making jam.

EAT, DRINK AND BE MERRY

Gone are the dark days when there were few options outside of chips, or maybe a pizza in most Scottish towns. There are an increasing number of restaurants offering international foods as varied as Chinese, Mongolian and Malaysian. Italian, Indian and kebab cafés tend to be the most prolific. Most restaurants have a vegetarian menu and some are entirely turned over to non-meat eating.

Tipping varies from place to place. Some include an obligatory 10 per cent, clearly marked on the bill at the end of the meal. However, most rely on the discretion of the customers and 10 per cent of the price of the meal is considered acceptable. Catering staff are notoriously underpaid and poorly treated in Scotland, so tips are always very welcome. Most restaurants stop serving at 9:00 pm and some keep their kitchens open until 10:00 pm, but seldom any later.

List of Typical Scottish Dishes

- Scottish breakfast: Traditional fried breakfast with a Scottish twist: *haggis*, black pudding and a potato scone
- Porridge: Hearty oatmeal dish that stops hunger in its tracks
- *Kippers*: Hot smoked herring
- *Arbroath smokies*: Smoked haddock
- *Kedgeree*: Smoked haddock, egg and rice curry
- *Cock-a leekie* soup: classic chicken winter warmer
- Scotch broth: Mutton stock, pulses, barley and vegetable medley
- *Cullen skink*: Smoked haddock, potatoes and cream
- *Haggis*: National talisman, not for the faint hearted. Usually served with 'clapshot', a mix of potatoes and turnips
- Venison stew: Unforgettably rich mix of gravy, venison and root vegetables
- Roast grouse: Local game bird, oven roast and served on a piece of toast
- Trout in oatmeal: Trout fried or grilled in oats and butter
- Fish and chips: No outing to the coast is complete without a 'fish supper'
- *Stovie*: Potato and onion mash fried up with minced beef or spam
- Pie: Pastry casing filled with hot fillings such as mince, cheese and onion, macaroni cheese and even potato, beans and sausage. More traditional meat pies include the scotch pie (hard pastry case) and the *bridie* (flaky pasty crescent)
- Oatcakes/*bannocks*: Classic oatcake biscuit, to die for with butter and heather honey
- Scone: Savoury cake that works wonders with cream and jam
- Shortbread: Buttery finger that melts in the mouth, or melts teeth in the mouth if you eat too much of it
- *Clootie* dumpling: Traditional Christmas cake made with dried fruits
- *Cranachan*: Oatmeal, cream and Drambuie

FOOD SHOPPING

Supermarkets and busy urban lives mean that people tend to put less time into cooking well-thought-out meals with local ingredients. The popularity of the vast selection of packaged meals available in most supermarkets is evidence enough that the same care and time isn't put into cooking these days.

Supermarkets that set up shop on the outskirts of the towns draw trade away from small local outlets. The local butcher and fruit and vegetable shops have had to contend with cheaper and more convenient shopping in the big supermarkets. But in more isolated country areas, the general store is still the local community's lifeline. Often housing the post office as well as provisions and newspapers, the village shop is the focal point of both trade and gossip.

WHISKY

No other spirit is so intimately connected to the spirit of a nation. After all, a bottle of whisky is—with the exception of men in skirts—the first thing that comes to mind when one thinks of Scotland. It is also the nation's primary earner, providing a big boost in exports to the British economy as a whole. It's not surprising that old, limited edition bottles can go for up to £ 2,000 a throw.

Despite some of the crazy prices on some bottles of malt whisky, its mystique is far more than just clever marketing. It is, after all, made up from Scotland's primal elements—barley from the earth, water from the rivers and streams, fire to malt the yeast and the damp, pure Highland air that matures the whisky through heavy oak casks.

Moreover, the mystery of its creation is uniquely Scottish. No other country in the world that has attempted to use the same ingredients and techniques to distil their own whisky has come anywhere near to the taste and quality of Scottish whisky. The Spanish, Germans, Americans and Japanese have all tried with limited degrees of success. But then much of a whisky is in its obscure Gaelic names such as Balvenie, Lagavulin or Laphroaig, so often mispronounced by visiting tourists. The Spanish imitation, called Dick whisky, hardly swings it. Only the Irish, so close in geography and spirit to Scotland, can match Scottish whisky in quality.

Many Scots say the magic that makes their whisky better than anyone else's is in the water from their Highland rivers. Although there is no evidence to support this, the word for whisky itself has root in the old Gaelic term for water, *uisge*. *Uisge beatha*, meaning the water of life, is the Gaelic term for whisky. Perhaps there is something to the praise muttered between sips, "Ah, 'tis the water of life."

It is thought that Saint Patrick from Southern Scotland brought the early knowledge of whisky distilling from Ireland around the mid-5th century ad. Knowing they were onto a good thing, the art of whisky production was kept a closely guarded secret by the early Christian monastic community right into the 15th century when the first written record pops up of its use for 'medicinal purposes'. From then on, whisky became a domestic affair with most Scottish homes brewing their own versions.

It wasn't until the 1840s that whisky's potential as a big earner was realised and big distilleries were built to produce it on a grand scale. They never looked back. Today, whisky is one of the top five UK export earners, competing with cars, aircraft, oil and the computer industry on the export market. If you buy a £ 12 pound bottle of whisky in Britain, around £ 8 pounds of that goes to the taxman. It's said that all the gold bullion in London doesn't add up in value to the whisky reserves in Scotland. Better still, whisky directly employs 14,000 people north of the border, with a further 47,000 people involved indirectly in the industry.

Malts Versus Blended

Whisky is a good thing all round for the Scots, but drinking it is not without its pitfalls for the uninitiated. To start with, there are whiskies and there are *whiskies*. Much is made of the difference between a standard blended whisky—or scotch—and it's finer cousin, the fine single malt.

The blended whiskies, which make up most of the exports, are standardised by being mixed together to produce a cheaper and more predictable result. The single malts are produced from one distillery and matured for a minimum of ten years in oak casks. The difference in quality and price between a single and a blended whisky is put down to the

distinctive flavour of each malt that comes from the particular water and air of each distillery.

Whether you drink a blended or single malt depends on the occasion. The good blended whiskies, such as Bell's and Famous Grouse are the work horses that oil the cogs of daily living in Scotland. These blends make up the standard fare in pubs, often drunk neat with a beer—this is known as a 'chaser'—or mixed with coca-cola or with ginger wine—a 'whisky Mac'.

A bottle of blended whisky, or 'the creature' as my Scottish uncle used to call it, sits in a cupboard in most Scottish homes to be dipped into on a cold night or when friends or family are around.

The versatile whisky even doubles up as medicine for mild ailments. Mixed with hot water, honey and lemon (known as a hot toddy), it is used as a cure-all from colds and flu to a warmer after a long day out on the hill. It may also be rubbed neat on baby's gums to deaden the pain from new teeth coming through, as well as giving them a lifelong taste for the milk of the motherland.

It is also seen by many as an essential tonic to ease the pains of old age. 99-year-old Lord Shinwell suggested introducing whisky into the House of Lords, that domain for ageing aristocracy, as a legitimate expense with the claim that, "...many of them cannot do without it because it is in the nature of a medicine." Shinwell also tried, and failed, to make blended whisky available on the National Health Service.

The malt whiskies, on the other hand, have an air of the sacred about them, although this can often have more to do with clever marketing than the quality of the drink itself. Even the most discerning of wine producers are unlikely to go as far as describing their product as having: 'The aroma of diesel oil and tar, seaweed and iodine, fishing net and fishing boats', as Laphroaig whiskey claimed in an advertisement.

Stored in their tall cylinder boxes for months on end, malts are usually opened only on special occasions and even then just for a taster, or a 'wee dram'. Malt is typically the centrepiece of a toast. It is brought out to celebrate occasions such as the birth of a newborn baby, the parting of friends or the sealing of a business deal. Bringing out the malt is a ceremonious affair. It should never be asked for, only offered by the host.

Contrary to common perception, most Scots don't say 'a wee dram for the road' these days, having seen fellow countrymen doing it too often in films over the years. The term 'dram' has fallen out of favour now, and people prefer to measure their firewater in singles or doubles. The equivalent measurement for a dram is an old quarter gill, or in modern terms, a double.

A malt whisky should only be drunk out of a whisky glass and is never mixed with anything but pure water. Ice is definitely not allowed. So much as waving a bottle of coke near single malt will drain the blood from most Scots' faces. There are some that say that even adding water to a malt whisky is tantamount to sacrilege. But a little extra water—especially Highland water—has never done a whisky any harm, in fact it can often help to release the flavours.

Much has been written about malt whisky's differing flavours or 'characters'. The clearest distinction that can be made is between the mainland and island malts. The peaty water used in the islands is mixed with seaweed, bringing with it a more pungent and smoky character. Try one of the Isle of Jura malts, famed for their distinctive flavour.

In truth, much of the reams of literature on the back of whisky bottles is a fanciful mixture of hocus pocus and snobbery. Of course, whisky does vary widely from region to region and from distillery to distillery. But in the end, it all comes down to personal taste. When attempting to choose from the dazzling choice of different brands and blends, it's best to remember the old Scottish adage: there is no such thing as bad whisky, just good whisky and better whisky.

A Bottle of Bru

Distinctly, Scottish brews don't stop with whisky. As well as a number of Scottish beers and ales, such as McEwans and Tenants, the country has its own unique soft drinks, Irn Bru and Tizer. Someone told me that Scotland is the only county in the world where Coca Cola isn't the most popular national soft drink because the Scots prefer Irn Bru.

Both drinks' mix of glucose, flavourings, orange colouring and fizz is not for the fainthearted. In one of Billy Connolly's best gags, that most famous of Scottish comedians wakes up in the morning in his bathroom with one of the worst hangovers of his life after a heavy night drinking and laments, "Never again, Baccardi and Tizer!"

Irn Bru in particular holds a real soft spot in this nation's sentimental heart. There is something timelessly Scottish, and in particular Glaswegian, about a bottle of Bru. It's especially essential to the tradesman reading a copy of the *Daily Record* on a building site—his bum hanging out of his pants, a cigarette smoked down to the filter and a bottle of Irn Bru for company.

ENTERTAINING

Inviting people round to dinner tends to be a fairly serious affair. In Scotland, great pride is taken in the home, so the hosts will often make a big effort to impress on their guests just how smart, cultured or rich they are. It may not look as though they have made much effort at all but don't be fooled; considerable thought will have been put into making things look as though the evening has been casually thrown together without a care in the world.

Once you have accepted an invitation, it is rude to show up more than half an hour late. Bring a bottle of something alcoholic (usually wine) and give profuse praise to the food and the cook regardless of what it really tastes like. Although there is no need to send a thank you note, a telephone call to say thanks is expected. It is polite to return the favour and invite your hosts around for dinner some time in the near future. The Scots have a keen sense of reciprocity when it comes to invitations.

Saying grace before eating is still common amongst Scotland's older God-fearing citizens. This can be a simple 'Thank you for the food that is about to be eaten,' or a longer prayer to cure the ills of the world. There is nothing more embarrassing than being told that it is time to say grace after you have already started your soup. So it is best to delay starting the meal until you know what that household's etiquette is regarding grace.

If this is all too formal and too much like hard work, house parties, or 'drinks', tend to be much more relaxed. They are commonly thrown to celebrate birthdays, a move to a new place (called a house or flat warming), in the run up to Christmas or to say goodbye to someone. House parties follow predictable lines: booze, chat and occasionally dancing. People are expected to bring drinks with them, although the host also provides something, usually a lethal punch that virtually corrodes through the plastic cups it is poured into. Food is offered in the shape of bite-sized nibbles in little bowls.

Social interaction is generally carried out standing up and you will be expected to circulate around the room making small talk to as many people as possible.

Whereas in some countries everyone puts booze onto a communal table and help themselves to whatever they fancy, in Scotland, guests can be a little protective over their drinks, so be wary of drinking someone else's.

The dress code at both dinner parties and house parties is smart casual. This means making an effort without over dressing. Men are generally dressed in shirts and jumpers, no tie or suit. Women generally opt for long skirts and blouses.

Go for muted colours if you do not want to stick out like a sore thumb.

Occasionally, house or flat parties have 'fancy dress' themes. This means that you are expected to dress up in ridiculous clothes and be good-humoured about it. There is no shame in this and many partygoers go to great effort and expense to come up with inventive costumes. I remember a James Bond theme party where one man turned up dressed as an underwater frogman, complete with wet suit and scuba diving tank!

LEISURE AND ENTERTAINMENT

CHAPTER 7

'Westering home, and a song in the air,
Light in the eye, and it's goodbye to care.'
—Sir Hugh S Roberton,
Glaswegian conductor and composer, 'Westering Home'

THERE IS MUCH MORE TO SCOTLAND than mountains, lakes and the distant sound of the bagpipes. The country has a thriving arts and entertainment scene. Whether it be Edinburgh's crazy festival vibe, football or a good old-fashioned *ceilidh*, Scotland is on a high right now.

MUSIC

It's Friday night and we are in the Taybank Hotel, in the small Perthshire town of Dunkeld. The square room with a long L-shaped bar is shaping up for a big night, packed as it is with a mix of musicians, regulars and the odd passerby like myself.

The din of conversation dies down as a group of musicians settle down at a table in the middle of the room. There are fiddlers, guitarists, a girl with a round drum bound with animal hide called a bodhran, and an old man with an accordion (or squeeze box as it is commonly called). They kick off the session with a slow tune and pick up pace as the evening goes on. Others come and go as they please, picking up the guitars that hang on the walls to pitch in for a tune or two before going back to their drinks.

At the end of the night, the group plays the ferociously fast 'Hangman's Reel'. Everyone bursts into spontaneous applause before wandering out into the crisp autumn night. It's a familiar scene, repeated in bars up and down the country.

Folk music is alive and well in Scotland, particularly in the country. Most villages and towns in the Highlands have at least one local 'ceilidh band', and the music is popular with young and old alike. The cities are no exception, just ask around to find out which are the folk pubs and turn up to see a folk jam, or session as they are known in Ireland and Scotland alike. If you are lucky, you may see the tunes put to Gaelic songs. This is when the language truly comes into its own. The other option is to go to a *ceilidh* and dance to some of the reels yourself.

Bigger name bands advertise themselves in concert halls and clubs. Some bands such as Capercaillie have such a large following that they tour Europe and beyond. Others fuse folk music with other styles, with varying results. I have heard Celtic folk music blended with rave music, African rhythms and salsa. Like all music, Scottish folk music is constantly changing and adapting to modern influences.

Scotland's musical talent isn't limited to folk music. There is also a thriving contemporary music scene in Glasgow. With live music venues such as the 13th Note, King Tut's Wah Wah Hut, The Garage and Barrowlands, the city has plenty of space for up-and-coming bands to get themselves heard.

As a result, Glasgow boasts an impressive hall of fame over the past 20 years or so.

Scottish groups that have made names for themselves in Glasgow before hitting the big time include Franz Ferdinand, Snow Patrol, Travis, Hue and Cry, The Soup Dragons, Simple Minds, Texas, Del Amitri and Wet Wet Wet.

Edinburgh doesn't have the same pull for up-and-coming bands as Glasgow, mainly because it lacks the venues for them to play in. But it still boasts some success stories, such as the Bay City Rollers and more recently, Goodbye Mr MacKenzie and Finley Quaye.

Scotland has a healthy festival scene over the summer months. The largest by far is T in the Park, held over a long weekend in July in Perth and Kinross. The festival now hosts over 120 acts and attracts an audience of around 85,000 people. For those wishing to avoid the crush, there are also plenty of smaller 'indie' festivals held in rural areas across Scotland.

DANCE

Just as Scotland has a vibrant folk scene, it maintains strong links to the past through the dancing of reels. No one really knows when reels date back to, although it's thought they were around long before Christianity made it to the island.

Close to standing stones dating back 5,000 years in Orkney, they found carvings of chain figures not unlike the wheeling pairs of one of the most classic of dances, the foursome reel. What devilish combination of astronomy, worship and flirtation the dances were then used for is a mystery.

In the 16th century, the dance's pagan past was found so suspect by God-faring Calvinists that they tried to ban them altogether. Scottish dancing went on regardless, becoming more and more sophisticated as it drew on similar traditions in France and the Basque country. None other than Mary Queen of Scots is credited with introducing some of the reels to the Scottish court from France in the late 16th century.

Once a ceremonial affair reserved for big occasions such as weddings, the dancing of reels is now a popular past time. The best way to take part is to look out for a *ceilidh*.

Ceilidh is a Gaelic word, originally meaning 'a meeting in a neighbour's house for a night of conversation, music and storytelling'. Nowadays, it is a general knees-up to live folk music. You can find *ceilidhs* across Scotland throughout the year, although the season starts in earnest in late autumn and runs up until Christmas.

Many visitors that come to Scotland imagine *ceilidhs* to be very formal affairs, with participants dancing a series of set routines with measured precision. This couldn't be further from the truth. A *ceilidh* is a bawdy free for all where everybody drops their inhibitions and dances the night away with friends and strangers. The popular reels played at a *ceilidh*, such as the Eightsome reel, the Dashing White Sergeant and Strip the Willow, are easy to follow and the band usually takes dancers through the basic moves before setting out on each new tune. If you get it all wrong, don't worry, it's all part of the fun.

Nothing beats a good *ceilidh*. For a start, there are no age barriers and the crowd tends to be a mix of old and young alike. Kids, in particular, have a fantastic time. The atmosphere is very informal with none of the dress code or airs and graces of a Highland ball. The dancing matches the drinking—fast and furious. Before too long, the boys are asking all the girls up to dance to spin them off their feet, and everyone feels like friends. Right at the end, everyone locks arms in a huge circle and sings an impassioned 'Auld Lang Syne' before the final, reckless waltz.

The Highland balls, also held one night each year in the autumn, are very different to ceilidhs. These are much more exclusive affairs, with long lines of tradition and etiquette. Most who go are from well-established families from the upper classes. Entry to outsiders is by invite only and there is a strict dress code of black tie or kilt for gentlemen and an evening dress for the ladies. If your attire is not up to scratch, you will be turned away at the door.

Dancing at the Highland balls is also much more formalised. The evening begins with a sit-down dinner, after which couples book dances with each other on dainty little cards. The reels themselves tend to be more complex, such as the Hamilton House and the Reel of the 51st, and it's important to have some idea of what you are doing before taking to the floor. Despite all the added show, the spirit of a Highland ball is no different from that of a *ceilidh*—a magical occasion of dance and drink leaving you with tired legs and a soaring heart at the end of the night. The best known of the Highland balls are held in Oban, Skye and Inverness.

CLUBS

At the other end of the spectrum is that most modern of answers to traditional country dancing: club culture. There are plenty of different styles and venues to choose from in Scotland, ranging from the hyper cool dance clubs of Glasgow to downright tacky Madonna and Abba theme nights.

The rave culture with thumping techno music used to be a big part of the British scene. Although the rave scene has had its day, it is still common to take recreational drugs (such as cocaine, ecstasy and speed) during big nights out.

ART

The art scene in Scotland is thriving at the moment. For the past decade, the art colleges in Glasgow, Dundee and Edinburgh have drawn bright young talent from across Great Britain, making them cutting edge centres for contemporary painting, ceramics and sculpture.

Painting has drawn high acclaim in Scotland ever since Scottish Colourists, often called 'Glasgow Boys and Girls', painted landscapes, still-lifes and portraits with bright, vivid brush strokes. The Glasgow Boys and Girls were Glasgow-based artists that brought fresh vigour and innovation in painting sculpture and decorative art between 1895 and 1920. Influenced by major movements of the time, such as Art Nouveau, Impressionism, Cubism and Expressionism, they made Glasgow a European centre for the arts until the focus shifted to Paris in the 1920s. Painters such as James Paterson, James Guthrie and James Nairn were known as the Colourists for their bright and vivid style. A few of the better known Glasgow Girls are Jessie Newbury and Frances MacDonald.

Today, the craft of painting is still alive and well in Scotland, despite much of contemporary art moving into video installations and conceptual statements.

Visit the Modern Art Museum in Glasgow and you will see the works of some of the big names of the past decade, like Peter Howson, Jack Vettriano and Ken Currie. Their big canvases explore darker impulses of intolerance and xenophobia, as well as modern secular religions such as football. John Bellany's watercolours and Jock McFadyen's sketches make up an eerie collection of portraits. Alison Watt and Jennifer Saville's portraits of women have also been very successful recently.

Sculpture in Scotland is no less exciting. A few names to look out for are Sir Eduardo Paolozzi's abstract pieces and, more recently, Kenny Hunter's work. Hunter's beautifully finished, life-sized plastic Christ can be seen at St Mungo's Museum of Religious Life and Art in Glasgow. It is also worth looking out for David Mach's Greek temples made out of tyres as well as Andy Goldsworthy's sublime workings of the natural environment.

The world of crafts is often overlooked in Britain, but is no less vibrant. In addition to native crafts such as basket weaving, there are strong glass and ceramic traditions in Scotland.

The big galleries in Edinburgh tend to draw the international art exhibitions. In recent years, the National Gallery, Portrait Gallery, Modern Art Gallery and Dean Gallery have held big retrospectives on the likes of Dali, Picasso, Klimt and Cezanne. Since devolution, these galleries have also had the purchasing power to buy paintings by old masters such as Murillo, Botticelli, Guercino and Canova.

THEATRE

Most people who know anything about the performance arts scene immediately think of the Edinburgh festival. This is hardly surprising as the three-week festival, running from the middle of August until the end of the first week of September, is the largest of its kind in Europe.

The atmosphere during the three weeks is electric. Edinburgh's population doubles in size as festival-goers flock to the city from around the world. The cafés spill onto the streets and the streets themselves become a spectacle. Walk down the Royal Mile any time of the day and you'll encounter a heady mix of dance, street performance, ticket touts in costume, hungover actors out of costume and a few fire jugglers to top it all off. That is, of course, if you can see your way through the bustle of the crowds.

The Edinburgh festival is also a focal point for dance, literature, storytelling, comedy and music from all around the world. But for all the festival's pomp and spectacle, its roots are in the fringe. The festival's fringe consists of small-scale, low-budget theatre, performed by anyone who has something to say and wants to say it to an audience. Buy a festival guide and you are immediately struck by the myriad of differing venues in attics and basements across town, each one offering radical new drama. This is true democracy: anyone who wants to can become a performer, regardless of how good or bad they are.

Here are a few key pointers to surviving the three weeks of late summer madness with your sanity and bank balance intact:

- Find somewhere to stay early. All the bed and breakfasts and hotels are often fully booked weeks in advance. If you have friends in Edinburgh that you can stay with,

Drumming up madness at the Edinburgh festival.

get really friendly with them well in advance: even floor space is at a premium.

- Try and be there for the first week of the festival (the third week of August). The first few days are the freshest and most exciting. By the end of the three weeks, the hectic atmosphere and cumulative hangovers have taken their toll on most festivalgoers.

- Don't just go and see anything that catches your eye and don't believe anything ticket touts tell you. If they are to be believed, every show in town is earth-shatteringly brilliant, when in reality many are far from it. There are plenty of student productions with more enthusiasm than talent. Gone are the days when a show cost two or three pounds and you could try your luck with some obscure theatre and still have change left for a few drinks afterwards. Nowadays, shows start at ten pounds, so it would be worth your while to do a little research. All the shows are extensively reviewed in the local and national newspapers, the official festival guide and the events magazine. However, reviews can also be unreliable, and at the end of the day, nothing beats a recommendation from someone you know or meet who has seen the show.

- Once you know what you want to see, make sure you buy your tickets in advance. The most popular shows, particularly in the bigger venues, sell out well in advance.

- Think twice before you go to the Military Tattoo. The Military Tattoo, for many the highlight of the festival, has been running for over 50 years now. The event is a colourful spectacle of Scottish military parades and dance troops from all around the world. The whole evening, rounded off with an impressive display of fireworks, is a time warp back to the grandiose days of empire and imperial rule. Some tourists can't get enough of it but others come away wishing they had spent their money elsewhere.

- Remember that the festival is as much about the atmosphere and the street life as the shows. You are likely to see just as much sitting in a café and watching the world pass you by as paying to go to the theatre. All the bars and cafés are open for most of the night during the festival, so bring headache pills and don't expect to get much sleep.

By the last day of the festival in September, everything transforms. Summer ends abruptly, the visitors depart en masse, and the city's residents come out of hiding to reclaim the streets.

For all the post-festival sobriety, the world of theatre continues apace across Scotland. The bigger theatres tend to show less contemporary, more classical theatre. The audience is expected to be well turned out and to turn up on time. Many productions close their doors at the starting time, regardless of whether or not latecomers have tickets. The smaller venues host more experimental theatre productions and are much more informal.

LITERATURE

There is a rich literary tradition in Scotland, made all the richer by the diversity of expression available to native scribes. After all, where most writers have full command of one language, many Scottish writers have grown up with Scots, Gaelic and English to choose from.

Celtic folk have also never been short of a story or two. Gaelic has always been an oral rather than a written language. So myths and legends were traditionally passed on from generation to generation in stories and especially in song. Old 'waulking songs' as they are called, tell tales of men going off to the galleys, raids between the clans and of course stories of love found and lost. Many of these tales have made rich pickings for modern writers and the art of telling them orally lives on to this day.

Scottish literature tends to explore a number of interrelated themes. The following brief description of some of these themes should help send avid bookworms out on the long winding road of Scottish writing.

The Historical Novel

The historical novel was first developed during the second and third decades of the 19th century (known as the Scottish Enlightenment) by the likes of Sir Walter Scott. Since then, truthful historical settings have been blended with fictional characterisation to tell rich and informative tales.

Sir Walter Scott is undoubtedly the best known author of the Scottish Enlightenment. His epic novels, such as

The Heart of Midlothian, are among the best examples of imagined characters rooted in historical fact. Although more renowned as a poet, James Hogg, a contemporary of Scott, explored the bloody aftermath of the Battle of Culloden in *Three Perils of Women*.

A number of historical novels were written in the last century, many of them touching on life in the Highlands before and after the clearances. Iain Crichton Smith's first novel *Consider the Lilies* is a beautifully considered portrait of an old lady's last days in her croft before she was evicted by the Duke of Sutherland to make way for sheep. Louis Grassic Gibbon wrote a wonderful fictional trilogy of books, *Sun Set Song*, *Cloud Howe* and *Grey Granite*, about rural life in the north-east of Scotland. Of the three books, I think that *Sun Set Song* best captures a sense of the period and its landscape.

A Ripping Yarn

For a sea-faring people, stories of adventure and intrigue have always come easily. Many of the best remembered Scottish authors told 'ripping yarns', high-spirited and fast-moving adventure stories that have kept their appeal through the ages.

The best known stories by Scottish authors have to be Robert Louis Stevenson's *Treasure Island* and Sir Arthur Conan Doyle's *Sherlock Holmes* novels. Compton Mackenzie's *Whisky Galore* is a classic fictional account of the disappearance of the shipwrecked SS Politician's precious cargo in the island of Eriskay. *Whisky Galore* was made into a film of the same name and another of Mackenzie's novels, *The Monarch of the Glen*, has recently inspired a BBC television drama. John Buchan's adventures of Richard Hanney, (the man who knew too much) in *The Thirty Nine Steps* also made it to the big screen, twice! In recent years, the *Harry Potter* series has been enormously successful, shooting its author J K Rowling to fame and fortune. The stories of one boy's fantastic adventures are meant for children but like all good children's books, are just as popular with grown ups.

The Supernatural

It is hardly surprising that so many Scottish authors and poets would take an interest in metaphysical worlds beyond the one we can see and touch. Myths, fairies and other fancies have always been a part of Celtic people's imaginings.

Fictional encounters with the supernatural date back to before the mid-18th century. Robert Burns' comic masterpiece *Tam O'Shanter* tells of a dark encounter with witches on the road home from the pub. James Hogg's *The Private Memoirs* and *Confessions of a Justified Sinner* explores the supernatural and is considered by many to be the best Scottish novel to date. Robert Louis Stevenson's *Dr Jekyll and Mr Hyde* needs no introduction.

More recent literature that touches on mythic spaces includes Neil Gunn's superb *Highland River* and *The Green Isle of the Deep*. George Mackay Brown's poetry and novels are also sumptuously strange, such as his saga-like collection of poems *The Wreck of the Archangel*. Perhaps Alasdair Gray's *Lanark* also fits into this category, with his surreal evocation of a parallel city to Glasgow.

Social Realism

In recent times, authors have been keen to move away from old fables and the romance of bonnie Scotland of tartan and the bagpipes. Many have preferred to concentrate on the grimmer realities in Scotland of poverty, urban deprivation and frustrated, failed lives

James Kelman, recognised as one of the finest 20th century Scottish writers, was at the forefront of focusing on the modern urban reality. One of his best known novels, *A Chancer*, plots the decline of a compulsive gambler. Alan Spence's *Its Colours They are Fine* is about the life and times of a Glasgow man. William McIlvanney's *The Big Man* is a tender portrayal of working class life in Glasgow. George Douglas Brown's *The House with the Green Shutters* is another excellent, if depressing read.

Tartan Noir

There has been a recent explosion of new Scottish writing much of it dark, humorous and violent. Much of this writing, known as *tartan noir*, is a kind of literary equivalent to the Quentin Tarentino film *Pulp Fiction*, only in a Scottish setting. It's a lost world of drugs, moral confusion and sudden death that reflects a very modern landscape.

The best known of this genre has to be Irvine Welsh's *Trainspotting*, an exploration into Edinburgh's underworld of drug addiction and poverty. *Trainspotting* is one of the few examples of cinema doing a novel justice. Glasgow writer Christopher Brookmyre's *The Country of the Blind* is another sassy venture into the darker sides of the human condition. Alan Warner's *Morvern Callar* is another classic of this genre.

Iain Banks has become something of a phenomenon in the past few years. Since his explosive debut with *The Wasp Factory*, he has produced a stream of excellent novels at a consummate pace, many of them science fiction. I think his best to date are *Complicity* and *The Crow Road*. Ian Rankin, also writing under the pseudonym of Jack Harvey, has made a name for himself for his well-crafted detective novels such as *Set in Darkness*.

Poetry

Poetry is impossible to pin down into a series of neat categories; it stands in the valley of its own making. Many of the authors mentioned above are or were poets and countless others have rhymed or sung their way into people's hearts. There is no point in attempting to list them all here but a few of the big names are Edwin Muir (also a novelist), Sorley Maclean, Norman MacCaig, Ian Chrichlan Smith, Edwin Morgan and, of course, Robert Burns.

THE PRESS

Britain's national press has traditionally taken little real interest in Scotland. However, since devolution, the British papers have been quick to catch up, now producing Scottish editions to keep pace with the country's new political life.

The five London-based broad sheets that cover Britain daily are *The Guardian* (comfortably left), *The Times* and *The*

Telegraph (predictably right), *The Independent* (tries to be true to its name) and *The Financial Times* (emphasis on business). Of these, *The Financial Times* and *The Guardian* tend to have the best foreign news.

There is a big tradition across Britain of buying the Sunday papers on lazy Sunday mornings and pouring over them whilst drinking endless cups of tea. Most of the papers do big Sunday editions with travel sections for sun-soaked daydreaming. *The Observer* is one of Britain's oldest newspapers and only comes out on Sundays. In Scotland, you can also choose from *Scotland on Sunday*, *The Sunday Herald* or the much-loved *The Sunday Post*.

For a spicier slant than the erudite tones of broadsheets, try one of the tabloid papers. These are the newspapers that dish the dirt; sex scandals, celebrity gossip and the other sensational stories. The Scottish versions of the British tabloids are *The Daily Star of Scotland*, *The Scottish Daily Mail*, *The Scottish Express*, *The Scottish Mirror* and *The Scottish Sun*.

Scottish news has long been covered in the country's three national publications: Glasgow-based *The Herald*, Edinburgh-based *The Scotsman* and Aberdeen-based *The Press and Journal*.

All the regions in Scotland are also well represented by local papers that mix local events with the bigger picture. For example, Edinburgh has the *Edinburgh Evening News*, Glasgow the *Daily Record*. Aberdeen's *Press and Journal* is particularly good. It is also well worth looking out for the feisty little west coast paper, the *West Highland Free Press*.

Go to a magazine rack in a newsagent and pretty much everything on offer is produced outside of Scotland. In such a small country, there just isn't the domestic market to publish a broad range of Scotland-specific material. One notable exception is the long running *Scottish Field*, a glossy magazine promoting country living for the stalking, shooting and fishing sect.

For an alternative take on the mainstream news, check out the *Big Issue*, sold by homeless people to help them make a living. Edinburgh's *Product Magazine*, available at arts centres, is also a good buy for a more artsy read.

TELEVISION

Britain prides itself on its high quality television. Old classics such as *Fawlty Towers*, *Dr Who* and BBC documentaries are still broadcast across the world.

There are five main channels to choose from, screened across the British Isles. BBC 1 and 2 come without adverts. ITV, Channel 4 and Channel 5 have advertisements.

With the advent of new technologies, there is now much more choice than before. Cable and digital television companies can hook you up to over 20 news programmes, sports and movie channels, as well as online shopping facilities.

Scottish television is increasingly finding its feet in the age of devolution. Scottish Television (STV) screens a fair amount of home-grown material while the BBC's flagship 'Alba' television channel broadcasts exclusively in Gaelic.

Scottish news is well covered by a number of stations, most of them based in Glasgow. However, exclusively Scottish BBC news is yet to come as the broadcasting rights remain in London.

CALENDAR OF FESTIVALS AND HOLIDAYS

This can only be a brief and inadequate guide to the biggest events in the Scottish calendar. Every city town and village has its own round of festivals and traditions which are best sought out locally.

- 31 December—Hogmanay
  This was originally an old Celtic festival to hasten back the sun, and until recently was more important than Christmas. It's now a massive knees-up held to usher in the New Year.
- 25 January—Burns Night
  A celebration of Scotland's principal bard Robert Burns.
- January—Shetland Islands 'Up Helly Aa' Festival
  This two-week festival celebrates the Isles' Old Norse heritage and ends with the traditional burning of a Viking longship and a torchlight procession through the streets of Lerwick.
- 14 February—St Valentine's Day
  A chance to send anonymous cards filled with love or lust to long-term partners and potential suitors. This is a

particularly charged day at school with kids comparing cards, trying to guess who sent them and seeing who got the most.

- March/April—Easter

  The Christian celebration of Jesus' resurrection. The date varies as it depends on the phases of the moon rather than the solar calendar. Like most of the religious festivals in Scotland, Easter has pre-Christian origins. The word 'Easter' also comes from the Celtic goddess of light and spring. The tradition of giving chocolate Easter eggs, symbolising new life, dates back to older pagan spring festivals. In an increasingly secular society, the religious significance of Easter is less important than it used to be. It is first and foremost a public holiday, running from Good Friday to Easter Monday.

- 1 April—April Fool's Day

  April Fool's is worth mentioning as it has caught out many an unsuspecting visitor. Called 'hunt the gowk' in Scots (the nearest translation is 'fool'), the first of April is a day for people to play practical jokes on each other. These jokes can be very elaborate. Back in the 1970s, the British Broadcasting Corporation (BBC) duped the entire nation by running a documentary on Italian spaghetti farming, complete with footage of the farmers picking strands of pasta off spaghetti 'trees'.

- Spring—Common Riding/Riding of the Marches

  This is a uniquely Scottish practice where the inhabitants of local areas ride out to the perimeters of their old 'burghs' to assert their identity. The dates and ceremonies, such as mock battles, vary from town to town, but most of the common riding is on the borders with England. The Selkirk Riding commemorates the Battle of Flodden back in 1513 against the English.

- 1 May—International Workers Day, known as May Day

  Big processions are held in the cities—the largest in Glasgow—to show solidarity with workers across the globe.

- 1 May—Beltane Fire Festival

  Traditionally a Celtic fire festival to celebrate the Celtic New Year. Many towns and villages across the country still light big bonfires on high points after nightfall. In ancient times, Celtic druids believed the dew before dawn on the morning after Beltane was sacred. Many still wash their faces in this dew on Arthur's Seat in Edinburgh in the hope that it will give them eternal youth.

- 12 July—The Orange Marches
  Held in Glasgow, the Protestant Orange Order marches through town to remind the Catholics who's in charge.

- August/September—The Highland Games
  The most famous games are held at Aboyne, Braemar, Glenfinnan, Inverness and Crieff.

- 10–30 August—The Edinburgh Festival
  Europe's biggest arts festival includes theatre, comedy, dance, music, film, literature, military tattoos and more. Be sure to find accommodation well ahead of time, the city gets so crowded that it's hard enough finding six feet of floor space, let alone a bed!

- 31 October—Halloween
  Christian festival All Saints' Day doubles up as a chance for kids to dress up as ghosts and ghouls to extort sweets off hapless pensioners.

- 5 November—Guy Faulkes Night
  A Britain-wide celebration of Guy Faulkes' death. Guy Faulkes was a 17th century anarchist who almost blew up the Houses of Parliament in London by stacking its basement with gunpowder. He was caught before he could ignite the fuse and burned at the stake, an event remembered with bonfires, the burning of effigies of 'The Guy' and lots of fireworks. The Scots have an ambiguous relationship with Guy Faulkes. Whereas in England, the night is a celebration of a catastrophe narrowly avoided, many in Scotland are more inclined to celebrate his near success. In truth, the events of the time are largely forgotten and it is more of an excuse to gather around a big bonfire on a chilly night, wave sparklers, set off fireworks and drink spirits to keep warm.

- 30 November —St Andrew's Day
  Scotland's national day and an occasion for the Scots to celebrate their patron Saint Andrew.

- 25 December—Christmas, celebrating the birth of Jesus
  Christmas comes early in Scotland. From the middle of November, the shops start decking themselves out in tinsel and fake snow, preparing for the shopping onslaught as everyone goes hunting for presents. The pubs fill up in the days running up to Christmas and the restaurants do a roaring trade hosting a seemingly endless round of work parties. It is also a time for amorous advances and minor indiscretions. So if someone approaches you with a sprig of a plant with white berries around Christmas, brace yourself. It's mistletoe and tradition has it that whoever stands under it has to kiss.

  Christmas is also an important time to get in touch with friends and family. It is customary to give a Christmas card to practically everyone you know. Most people spend the big day itself with their family. St Nicholas, or Santa Claus, pops down chimneys to fill big stockings at the end of children's beds with presents the night before. Presents are also laid out under the Christmas tree and traditionally opened after lunch, if everyone can wait that long. Christmas dinner is a huge feast of turkey, vegetables, and roast potatoes. Christmas Mass is most commonly held at midnight before 25 December.

THE GREAT OUTDOORS

A low slanting October sun floods into the glen. It lights up the countryside like it's one of those romantic last scenes of a movie where the hero strides off into a brightly painted sunset. The bracken is lit a rusty orange, the grass seems to be on fire, the birch trees shimmer with greens and yellows, and the berries on the rowan trees are a deep glowing red. The sky beyond is black with rain and a passing rainbow showers down curtains of colour. We walk on knowing that every bend on the winding track out of Glen Affric will bring fresh wonders.

In a world increasingly choked with traffic, noise and pollution, much of Scotland offers a wonderful contrast. It has rainbows, clean running rivers, space to breathe and a magical silence. There is something of every northern country about the thin light and water-rich lands, but Scotland is unique, holding a timeless mystery. No other countryside I've seen has touched me in quite the same way.

It is not surprising that the country has become such a haven for outdoor types. Most settle for hillwalking, ranging from short easy treks to the restless search for windswept mountain peaks. Walking alone is not always enough. The Scots have also found all kinds of ways of entertaining themselves while they walk through the countryside. Hitting a small ball with a stick and shooting or stalking wild game comes immediately to mind.

But there is more. 'Scotland offers unlimited options for leisure,' touts one local guide book. So then, just what are all these leisure options and are they really unlimited?

Hillwalking and Climbing

Hillwalking or climbing can be physically demanding, but travelling through Scotland's wide-open spaces on foot is definitely well worth the blisters. In many ways, this simplest of outdoor pursuits in Scotland is also one of the most satisfying. No other means of travel gives you the time to soak in and appreciate the beauty of your natural surroundings.

Much of this popularity is due to the unprecedented freedom of access walkers in Scotland enjoy. Unlike England, which has strict trespassing laws, Scotland is wide open to walkers and climbers alike. You can pretty well chart your own route through the glens and to the top of the mountain of your choice.

The only exception is during the deerstalking season, when walkers can scare off the prey and put their own lives at risk from stray bullets. If you are setting out for anywhere high and wild from September through November, call the local estate to see if they are stalking. Sundays are rest days for stalkers and deer alike.

Climbing mountains in Scotland is often called 'walking the hills'. Don't be confused into thinking that these are gentle ambles, they are real mountains and real challenges. Walking the hills in Scotland has its own terminology. People don't walk or climb up mountains in Scotland, they 'bag Munros'. A

Munro refers to a mountain with a height of over 915 m (3,000 ft). Munros are named after Sir Hugh Munro who famously charted the hundreds of high peaks in Scotland in the early part of the 20th century.

To 'bag' a Munro, you have to climb it and touch the pile of stones, or cairn, at the top before moving swiftly onto the next one. Some turn this practice into a kind of personal trial, seeing how many Munros they can bag in a summer.

Calling a mountain a 'Munro' isn't the only source of confusion when it comes to navigating your way across Scotland on foot. Gaelic names for hills, lakes, streams and more besides add to the Scottish landscape's distinctive romance. The very sound of the valleys and villages conjures up a lyrical charm: Kinlochleiven, Achlachan moss, Rubha Ruadh.

For those who wish to set a more leisurely course to a mountain top, there are countless well-marked nature trails across Scotland that cater for both day-trippers and hardcore backpackers. Most famous of these are the Southern Upland Way and the West Highland Way. The Southern Upland Way runs 341 km (211.9 miles) from the west coast in Portpatrick to the Cockburnspath on the Berickshire coast south of Dunbar. The West Highland Way starts in Milnagavie just North of Glasgow and finishes up some 152.9 km (95 miles) North in Fort William. Many finish off the Highland walk by walking up Scotland's highest peak, Ben Nevis, which looms out of the spectacular scenery of Glen Coe. Leaflets of outings, walks and trails are available from local tourist information centres.

Many come to see the wild life that inhabits this land of mountain, sea and rainbows. Bird watchers, with their array of binoculars and bird identification books, are in paradise. There is nothing more arresting than a glimpse of majestic golden eagles making lazy circles high in a mountain pass. There are reportedly only 160 nesting pairs left in Scotland. Rarer still is the capercaillie, an elusive woodland bird with a shrill, distinctive call. Few ever see a capercaillie, which now faces extinction due to growing pressure on its woodland habitat.

Scotland is also a popular destination for migratory birds, especially feathered escapees from winters in Iceland and Greenland. Look out for ducks, coots, geese, rare swans such as the mute and whooper, waders, grebes, oyster catchers and ringed plovers. For novice 'birdies' like myself, nothing beats the long call of oyster-catchers as they lift gracefully off the incoming wash of a sandy beach with a flash of orange beaks.

Land and sea mammals are also abundant. Many of the beasts still found in the wilds of Northern Scandinavia, such as wolves, bears and wild boars, have long since disappeared. However foxes, hairy mountain goats and deer still stalk the land. Along the coasts, there are colonies of seals with their big watchful eyes and a few extremely shy sea otters. Marine tourism is also on the rise. Tour operators offer trips to see dolphins, porpoises, puffin colonies and minkie whales.

Scotland isn't a leisure park and exploring it can be risky. Much of the country is wild and barren and every year, walkers and climbers lose their way down ravines or off cliffs. Most notorious is Ben Nevis, Scotland's highest mountain. In the winter, the routes up are treacherous. I remember reading in one particularly cold winter how 15 people hadn't made it off the 'hill' alive. Just outside Tyndrum in the Central

Safeguards

When setting out hillwalking, it's best to keep in mind the following safeguards:

- Check the weather reports. Forecasting the weather, which can change rapidly, is a notoriously unreliable science in Scotland. The Mountain Rescue Service provides a regularly updated report that is better than most. There are also avalanche watches in spring, which divert climbers and walkers away from black spots.
- Let someone know of your intended route and when you expect to be back.
- Take a map and compass and don't change your route along the way.
- Don't go on your own.

Highlands, a roadside cairn is dedicated to the hundreds of walkers who have died in the Cairngorm Mountains in the last century. The cairn, built from stones taken from the tops of over four hundred surrounding mountains, reads, 'They died in a place they loved.'

The Mountain Rescue Service in Scotland is famed for the lives it saves every year. Too many people get into trouble because they aren't well prepared. The trick is to be ready for every eventuality. As well as the regular hillwalker's clobber such as good boots and a tent, you need waterproofs from head to foot, shorts, sunglasses, sunscreen, warm clothing, windproof hats and scarves. A day out can feel like a constant striptease as you juggle the layers between hot, wet and biting cold.

Wild Weather

I remember walking up a hill by Loch Hourn on the west coast one unexpectedly warm September day. It was a bright autumn day and the view was fantastic. Not that it made much impression on us as we trudged up the path weighed down by several layers of clothes—thermal underwear, two jumpers, a wind stopper and a heavy waterproof. I felt like a human boiler, letting off puffs of steam like some overheated cartoon character.

When we reached the top of the hill, everything about the weather changed in an instant, clouding over and pouring down first rain, then sleet, then snow. With visibility down to a just few feet, we crouched by a big stone for protection, disorientated and assailed by the elements. In a country of sudden contrasts, foul weather can regularly gatecrash on a sunny day only to evaporate just as quickly as it appeared.

Good orienteering skills are just as important as equipment. A map and compass are essential for long walks that don't follow well-marked paths. Ordnance Survey, or OS maps as they are commonly called, are available in most bookshops and tourist offices. They provide detailed and extensive coverage of Scotland's every nook and cranny.

Do not think that taking a mobile phone is a substitute for wandering off poorly equipped. In the last couple of years, the mountain rescue has been inundated with calls from disorientated walkers stuck on mountains with little more

than a pair of flip flops and a T-shirt. Go prepared and don't cry wolf just because you have a cell phone and know that you can.

Of course, meticulous precautions and planning can go too far. I remember a couple of professional-looking hillwalkers mapping out their day's route. Dressed impeccably for the hill, they were taking no chances. They had bright Gore-Tex clothes, head torches, gleaming boots, ice axes, and ski poles to aid balance. They stood pouring over a detailed laminated map setting compass bearings for the top of the nearby mountain. What confounded the scene was the absence of snow and the big signpost that they stood next to clearly pointing out the path that led straight to the peak.

Stalking and Shooting

If climbing, walking or driving through nature isn't entertaining enough, you can always opt to stalk it. 'Stalking, shooting 'n fishing' is an ancient pastime in Scotland that still holds immense appeal.

Wild animals have provided an essential source of protein to the Scots from the earliest times when the Pictish people hunted deer by driving herds of them off cliffs. Discarded deer bones have been found in settlement remains dating back 7,000 years.

With the advent of supermarkets, shooting and stalking wild game has long since become a recreational sport. And yet it is more than a sport. It is a kind of ritual, tied up with tradition, social custom and controversy. Getting involved takes much more than a steady aim, you have to also be sensitive to the currents that underlie the sport itself.

The term 'stalking' in Scotland refers to hunting deer with high-powered rifles. Shooting describes shooting grouse with shotguns. Fox hunting with dogs on horseback is also a popular pastime in Britain. Fox hunting in Scotland, however, does not extend far beyond the borders with England where it is most commonly practised.

Stalking and shooting is carried out on the big estates. These estates own huge tracts of Scotland, which they maintain for sheep farming and blood sports. This means that civilisation doesn't encroach on the deer's natural habitat of high moor. Moorland grouse also feed themselves on heather and every season, the old heath is burnt off to ensure fresh growth.

The red grouse lives in relative peace for most of the year in groups (or coveys) in deep heather. This all changes on 12 August (known as the glorious twelfth), when the hunting season for grouse is declared open across the country. Groups set out to walk over set areas (known as beats), shooting grouse that fly into their line of fire. Alternatively, some groups stand in wait in a small trench (known as a butt) to shoot grouse as they fly over. The grouse are driven over by beaters further down the valley. Gun dogs, mainly labradors, are used to flush out the birds, and then pick them out of the long heather after they have been brought down.

The members of the shooting party, or guns, break for a pack lunch in the middle of the day and then swing back for home, shooting as they go. At the end of the day, they compare their individual tallies, counted in pairs or braces, and comment on how the day went. A hundred years ago, thousands of grouse would be shot in a single day by a few guns. These days, disease, climatic change, and arguably overshooting, has taken its toll. Grouse populations are in gradual decline.

The king of all Scottish game beasts is in no such trouble. Red deer, native to Scotland, are so plentiful that they have to be culled each year to keep numbers down to a manageable level. Much of the Highlands are infertile high moor, and this is the habitat that is ideal for the herds of deer, that thrive in Scotland's bleak heights. They have done so well that overcrowding has left them 25 per cent lighter in weight now than they were 100 years ago. They are also much more prone to illness. Each year, the big estates are obliged to shoot hundreds of deer, usually picking off the old and infirm to keep numbers under control. Most of the stalking is done in the month of October.

Much of this task falls to the estate gamekeeper, particularly when it comes to shooting the hinds in the winter months. However, many sportsmen and women look forward to shooting stags during their mating season (or rut) in October. It is a skilful task, one that requires a lot of stamina.

The thrill comes from silently stalking a stag on your hands and knees, dressed from head to toe in camouflage to avoid being spotted. The gamekeeper, or stalker, is invariably on hand to help the shooter get to a hundred or so metres from the unsuspecting beast and to give the go ahead if he thinks it's a clear shot. There is no greater shame than wounding a beast and letting it get away.

Once shot, the deer is gutted, or 'gralloched', on the hill and then transported to the butcher. If the stag is a handsome beast and has an impressive set of antlers, he can look forward to having his head set on a plaque to be admired by future sportsmen and curious children. It's worth noting that when you shoot your first stag, or grouse for that matter, you can expect to have your face marked with the blood of your first kill. It's called being blooded.

After a stalking or shooting holiday, it is customary to tip the gamekeeper, after all, it was probably his or her skill that led you to your prey in the first place. Often struggling to make a living from hill farming during the rest of the year, tips are an important supplement to a gamekeeper's income. Expect to give between £ 20 and £ 50 a day for grouse shooting and about £ 50 for a day of stalking. It's best to give a tip discreetly, in the form of a handshake and an envelope.

The Sporting Estate

Blood sports in Scotland are traditionally reserved for the upper classes. Stalking and shooting became a popular pastime for the well-heeled in 19th century Victorian Scotland, after Queen Victoria fell in love with the Highlands and first leased the Balmoral estate in 1844. The estate remains a much-loved retreat for present-day royalty.

With the royal seal of approval, the pursuit of aristocratic blood sports became a litmus paper for high social standing. After centuries of indifference to the Highlands, rich industrialists from the South, British blue blood—and their money—flowed North.

Suddenly, deer stalking and grouse shooting was big business, bringing much needed income to the big estates at a time when rural Scotland was suffering from agricultural depression. The amount of estate

There is something oddly British about all that bruising physical discomfort and fortitude against capricious weather and rough ground. The old whisky-soaked, tweed-draped duffer, complete with pipe, red nose and his faithful dog, has become an enduring caricature of the Scottish Highlands.

An old shooting lodge in Perthshire.

land set aside almost exclusively for stalking and shooting increased dramatically. Between 1883 and 1912, the average estate size doubled and the Highlands were increasingly allowed to return to open moor as it is today, ideal for grouse and deer.

Many sporting lodges have changed hands in recent years. They have become increasingly expensive to run privately. Multinational companies have bought many sporting lodges to run as businesses for corporate entertainment. The big organisations concerned with conservation, such as The National Trust and the John Muir Trust, are also big landowners now. Only a few of the old estates remain in private hands.

Bloodsports are no less exclusive these days than in the 19th century. Expect to spend an average of £ 250 for each stag shot and up to £ 110 for a driven brace of grouse, and this is before counting accommodation and food.

There is a reassuring sense of tradition to a full day's shooting. On returning to a lodge after a day's shooting, hot baths are lined up, and everyone changes to more formal dress for the evening ahead. Tea and cake is served, followed a little later by drinks and then a formal three-course meal with all the trimmings. Dinner is usually a cheery and noisy affair of stories, jokes, speeches and toasts. And of course the port is passed around at the end of every meal.

The clothing required for stalking and shooting has changed little over the centuries. Standard uniform on the hill includes a checked shirt, a waxed jacket and often a cloth cap to complete the look. Men and women don plus-fours, which are tweed trousers that stop just below the knee. Long socks are pulled up over the calf to provide protection from the elements. Twenty-first century outdoor wear such as bright Gore-Tex jackets, is lost on this crowd who see it as being somehow impractical.

You will have probably noticed that women have had little mention in this section. Bloodsports are predominantly male dominated. This isn't to say that women are excluded; they aren't, and if they do take part, they are often the keenest shots. It's just that the sport has more appeal to the hunting instincts of men. Girlfriends, daughters and wives play the no less important role of making sure that their men don't take themselves, and their guns, too seriously.

Land and People

Stalking and shooting draw strong critics in Scotland and around the world. Talk to a cross section of society and you will hear passionate arguments for and against, but seldom indifference. It's not surprising, considering the sport is so intimately tied up with class, land, and ultimately politics.

The most emotive debate surrounds the issue of land. A few wealthy individuals have owned much of Scotland ever since the Norman conquerors first carved up the country for themselves in the 13th century. My own well-known Scottish name, Grant, comes from a family of French nobles called Le Grand who were given the area around Inverness to lord over. Eventually, they intermarried with the locals and went native. Patterns of land ownership have changed little since, with a few estates owning much of rural Scotland. Many feel resentful that the old estates cleared their tenants to make way for the more profitable sheep farming and blood sports.

Today's figures on land ownership speak for themselves. There are around 14 million acres of land in Scotland for a population of 5 million people. Of all this land, 1,252 landowners—0.25 per cent of the population—own over two-thirds of all the rural land.

Plenty of Scots would be happy to see an end to sporting estates, considered by many to be big playgrounds for the rich. Advocates of sporting estates are just as vocal. The pro-blood sports lobby points out that stalking and shooting brings essential cash and jobs to isolated areas of Scotland. Much of the land that makes it possible for deer to thrive is too poor to do anything else with apart from converting it into forestry plantations. The argument goes that it is the way the large estates manage their land that has conserved the natural beauty and wildlife that we have come to take for granted in Scotland.

And so the debates have gone round in circles for generations, although the tradition of sporting estates is somewhat on the back foot at the moment. With national parks now set up by the Scottish Executive in Loch Lomond and the Cairngorms, the pattern of land ownership may be set change. Fox hunting has also been banned, although stalking and grouse shooting are not threatened. It looks like 21st century issues are finally catching up with this most Victorian of pastimes.

FISHING

Salmon inspire awe and respect in equal measure from fishermen and women who cast their long lines into Scotland's rivers in the hope of landing one. Success is never assured as they are notoriously difficult to catch.

Salmon 'run' up Scotland's rivers from spring until late autumn. They spend the rest of the year fattening up in the Atlantic somewhere off the Greenland shelf. They travel up Highland rivers, covering up to 25 km a day, to spawn and return, or to die. The bigger, slow flowing peaty rivers in the east such as the Dee, Tay and the Spey offer the best fishing.

An Ode to the Mighty Salmon:
lonesome traveller
roaming your underworld
of rock and dark waters
jumping clear
of falling torrents
unhindered, unerred
in the pitch
of an ancient night

rested and yet restless
in your eddy
your backwater
of silvering light
a muddy shallow
from the ocean
that cradled you
destined to survive
a bony act of will
destined to die
exhausted on a
grassy bank
tricked by a feather
betrayed at dusk
floundered, sunk
on a quivering line.
lonesome traveller
your spirit merges
mountains with sea
the sky with this broken stream
and death with life
with life
itself

—Author

Salmon of all shapes and sizes swim up these rivers and are named according to their age or condition. The baby parr are no more than a few months old, the smolts are up to two-years-old, and a mature salmon lives until it is about six-years-old. A spent salmon, meaning a fish that has spawned and is heading back to sea, is called a kelt. To confuse matters even further, a male salmon is called a cock and a female salmon a hen.

Despite the best efforts of fishermen and scientists, the Atlantic salmon remains a mystery. No one knows for certain

Willie MacGregor, an experienced gamekeeper on a Highland estate best summed up what's known about these elusive creatures in his own inimitable style. He said, "If I wrote a book entitled *How Much I Know About Salmon Fishing*, by Willie MacGregor, the contents would be a single blank page." This is hardly surprising given that no one can even explain why salmon take the fisherman's fly in the first place as they don't eat a thing while coursing upstream to their spawning grounds.

why they search out exactly where they were born to return to and spawn again. Nor why they come into the rivers' lower reaches on a full moon's high tide. Experienced fishermen will even tell you that they even predict the weather, rushing through a shallow stretch of river just before a dry spell makes it impassable.

Environmental pressures increasingly threaten wild salmon. The number of salmon in Scottish rivers has been in steady decline since about a century ago when they were so plentiful that farmers used to feed them to the pigs.

Netting salmon in big numbers in sea estuaries has virtually stopped, and these days, many fishermen return their catches to the river, especially the hens. But the reasons for the salmon's decline are more complicated than just overfishing. Much of the blame has been placed on salmon farms polluting inshore waters with chemicals and spreading disease from farmed salmon to their wild cousins. Whatever the reason, the possibility of Scotland's rivers becoming empty of salmon, like many in England and North America, is no longer a remote one.

Fly-Fishing for Salmon

Fishing for salmon in Scotland with a small imitation fly on a long fly rod has been popular since the 19th century. Salmon are much easier to catch with live bait or a lure. In fact, poachers use everything from nets to poison to catch salmon in the dead of night. But it is fly-fishing that is considered the proper way to fish for salmon, and it requires great patience and skill.

The art of fly-fishing lies in pitting yourself against a prey that has even odds of getting away. It is a real contest, a battle of wills. There is a whole science to fly-fishing, with enough books written on techniques to clog up the very estuaries themselves. For more information on the finer points of different flies, casting and optimum light and weather conditions, please refer to the Further Reading at the back of this book.

One thing is for certain, being a good salmon fisherman, or woman, requires much more than skill and good luck. You need a reflective temperament to pass an often uneventful day by a quietly flowing river. One anonymous author writing on his passion best summed up the sports' job description, "The chief qualities required are patience, a love of nature to enable you to appreciate the surroundings and the bird life, keenness, and of course, plenty of time and complete disregard of the weather. Without this, you'll never be a fisherman."

It's funny the quote should end with the word 'fisherman' when many claim that women have the best luck. The record for the biggest salmon caught using a fly in British waters is held by a Mrs Morrison on the River Deveron in October 1924. The beast weighed an awesome 28 kg (61 pounds)! There is even a theory that female pheromones lure the salmon onto their lines, causing much chagrin amongst the fraternity of male fishermen.

Finding a spot to fish for salmon legally can be tricky as fishing rights in Scotland bear no relation to land ownership. Many sporting estates offer fishing as part of the shooting-stalking package mentioned above, but this is not guaranteed.

Most of the fishing is divided into beats, or stretches of riverbank, which are hired out in week-long blocks during the season. Established fishermen are offered the same beat year in and year out, making it hard for newcomers to find a space. Applying for a beat is a slow and complicated process that involves getting onto a tenancy list of a river's letting agent or proprietor.

The best bet is to get invited onto someone else's beat or to go directly to the river's gamekeeper, or *ghillie*, for a day's licence. Every salmon river has one or more *ghillies*. Their job is to husband the waters, watching out for poachers and limiting the number of fishermen on each stretch of water.

They also have an intuitive knowledge of their rivers' elusive travellers, offering advice on the best spots to fish and on the finer arts of actually landing one.

Salmon fishing isn't cheap. Catching a salmon on one of the big name rivers costs as much as £ 10,000 pounds! Fish one of the smaller rivers with less salmon and you can expect to pay between £ 12 and £ 80 for a day's licence.

Trout and Pike Fishing

Fishing for the salmon's poorer cousin, the humble brown trout, holds less appeal but can be just as satisfying. Where the salmon rivers are well managed and easily accessible, catching trout often just involves a long tramp up to an isolated river or loch. Trout may be smaller and easier to catch than salmon, especially if you use a spinning rod with a bright lure instead of a fly, but they are just as tasty.

In recent years, fisheries for the North American rainbow trout have sprung up, mainly on the borders and in central Scotland. For a fee, you can throw a fly in one of these small, well-stocked lakes with a greater chance of catching something than if you are fishing for the wilder and wilier brown trout.

Pike, denizens of the deep, are the ugliest fresh water fish in Scotland. The Endrick Pike Head on display at the Kelvingrove Art Gallery in Glasgow looks like a primitive version of the monster from the film *Aliens*. The head is all that's left of the 113 kg (70 pound) beast found in 1934. Pike are caught with a big lure, dead bait, or even a bit of cheese. They make for a smelly, bone-infested meal, but are tasty if eaten very fresh.

The closed season for trout in Scotland is from 7 October to 14 March, both days inclusive. Many areas extend these dates to give trout stocks more time to recover. Licences to fish trout or pike are much easier to get hold of than those for salmon fishing and are much cheaper. Most country hotels and tackle shops sell licences for between £ 5 and £ 25 for a day. A rod licence is not required in Scotland. The Orkney Isles is the only place where you don't need a licence, and can just cast a line into the waters.

GOLF IS GREAT

Walking across Edinburgh's central parkland, the Meadows, one winter evening, I saw a man holding a golf club in the half-light of a drizzly night gazing intensely at a point in the distance. He steadied himself and swung. The golf ball flew off and neatly landed a hundred yards on, between lamp posts and the folks walking home from work. The man cursed, set down another ball and thwacked it off again in the same uncertain direction, barely discernible in the failing light. There was something about the disregard the man had for the rain, the encroaching night or the people walking home liable to bizarre injury that sums up just how seriously golf can be taken in Scotland. And what better place to play if you have the itch.

Golf has been with Scotland for a very long time. In fact, Scots often make the proud boast that they invented golf. This isn't strictly true. Golf, or *kolf* as it was then termed, was a popular pastime among the Scots and Dutch. In medieval times, they aimed at specific trees for competition instead of thwacking balls down holes. Scotland was the birthplace of golf with holes in the ground as a target, and the rest is history...

The earliest written references to golf in Scotland date back to 1457, when King James banned the game (along with soccer) because it was keeping his subjects away from archery practice. Few people paid much notice though, and by the 17th century, the sport of golf was in full swing.

Most passionate golfers make the pilgrimage to St Andrews, a small and picturesque town in Fife on the East Coast. The Old Course running alongside the sea just outside the town is hallowed ground for golfers. Play there and you walk in step with most of the masters of the past. In June 2000, it was Tiger Woods' turn, winning the British Open competition on the Old Course with a typically comfortable margin. Some 80,000 fans turned out to watch.

Although there are golf courses scattered around Scotland, St Andrews remains the undisputed home of golf. Where else can they boast of no less than six courses, designed for varying levels of fitness and skill. St Andrews is also the

Beware, too much golf can be hazardous to your health!

home of the National Golf Museum, which holds a stunning array of glass cases filled with dissected golf balls. These displays offer detailed explanations of the advances in ball technology over the years.

There is much more to golfing in Scotland than just St Andrews. The variety of courses, usually set in breathtaking surroundings, makes the whole country a great draw for enthusiasts. There are the typical seaside links courses such as Troon, Dornoch, Nairn, Muirfield and Gullane. Parkland courses such as Pitlochry and Machrihanish offer a mix of trees, ponds and lakes. Then of course there are the Highland courses such as Gleneagles and Loch Lomond to add to the list.

Part of the appeal of golfing in Scotland is also the challenge. Wild weather and less manicured fairways makes the game more demanding but also more rewarding than in many other countries.

Golf in Scotland caters for every pocket. Expect to pay as little as £ 1.50 a round on one of the smaller courses in the low season and as much as £ 100 for a round on the most prestigious courses, such as the Old Course or Gleneagles.

The green fees for a round of nine or 18 holes is paid to a club's resident professional golfer in the pro-shop. You can buy equipment and hire clubs, buggies, manual trolleys or even electrical caddy carts there.

Caddies have to be booked in advance and are paid between £ 20 and £ 50 a round depending on their experience. If you play well and feel the caddy has been suitably encouraging, expect to give a tip of between 10 per cent and 25 per cent of his or her fee. Always give a note rather than loose coins.

Playing golf in Scotland if you are a complete newcomer to the game is not easy. Most clubhouses will not allow play unless the golfer has a handicap certificate. This is the average number of strokes it takes an individual to get around a course, over and above the course's par. To get a handicap, you have to join a golf club and have your ability assessed over a few rounds before being given a certificate. Even then, the most prestigious courses are often not for beginners. Men need to have a handicap under 24 and ladies under 36 to play the Old Course.

Becoming a member of a golf club in Scotland takes persistence. The first port of call is the club's secretary, who interviews prospective members. If you are deemed suitable, you will then be invited to apply, so it is important to humbly explain your motives for joining rather than bluntly declare that you wish to be a member. The next step is to find two existing members who are willing to propose and second your application. The more prestigious courses require up to ten members seconding an application.

Next, you will be asked to play a round of golf with at least two members. You have to demonstrate to them that you know the rules of the game and aren't completely hopeless on the course, holding everyone else up behind you. It is also important to show the right sporting spirit, not swearing blindly and tearing chunks out of the green if you miss a hit but saying things like 'good shot' when your opponent is making mincemeat of you.

Even if you jump all these hurdles, you may still have to wait. Many clubs have waiting lists that are up to 20 years long. In fact, some club members put their children down on the list when they are born, so that if they develop a passion

for the game, they can become club members themselves by the time they are 20.

Those who are invited to join are expected to pay twice the annual subscription as an entrance fee. Annual membership varies between £ 100 and £ 1,500 depending on the course, but after that, you can play as much as you like for no additional fee. Friends and family can play at discounted rates. You have to own your own golf clubs and shoes.

Traditions in golf are almost as important as the game itself in Scotland. So much so that each course has its own peculiarities. It's worth phoning a clubhouse in advance to find out if there are any surprises. For example, there are a few clubs that still admit men only, and the most prestigious can insist that visitors play with a member. To play a round on the Old Course, your name has to be picked out of a ballot on the morning that you are due to tee off.

Lunch is common to all of the clubhouses. In the 18th century, a three- to four-hour feast typically followed a round in the morning. Golf, business and eating were so interlinked in those days that members were fined if they didn't turn up to dine after playing.

These days the social side to golf isn't so strictly enforced but remains just as important. A round of golf, lasting an average of three hours, is usually played before or after lunch in the clubhouse. It is a good idea to choose and order lunch, even if it is only a sandwich, well in advance to avoid a long wait.

Dress sense is not as formal as in Victorian times when women wore long frocks and hats and men sported shirt and tie, a smart Norfolk jacket and cap. On the course, men and women are expected to wear a shirt with a collar and a pair of slacks. Jeans are not allowed. Most courses require spiked golf shoes that don't tear up the greens. The clubhouse's mixed bar and restaurant requires a jacket, shirt and tie for the men and equally smart attire for the women, usually a dress.

To this day, golf remains something of a man's world. Women used to be barred from most courses and a curt sign still reads 'No ladies or dogs' on the entrance to the Royal and Ancient clubhouse in St Andrews. Most clubhouses still have a men-only spike bar for drinks straight off the course. The ladies have to get changed first, before meeting up in the mixed bar later.

Although there are many keen lady golfers, the sport's traditional image of men with moustaches is hard to shake off. Nor is the attitude many older golfers have to the ladies. On being told that the men-only bar was to be done away with in his club house, one old timer said, "It's not the ladies that I object to, it's the bloody women."

Then there are those who object to the game itself. Ever since King James banned golf in favour of archery practice, golfers have been gently chided for 'ruining a good walk'. When I asked golf enthusiast Roger Wood, sadly no relation to Tiger Woods, what he had to say to those who thought that the whole business was an expensive waste of time, he leapt eloquently to the game's defence. "It's much more fun to practice mind over matter than to walk in a vacuum," he said.

A Brief Glossary of Golfing Terms

Albatross	Extremely rare just like the bird, this denotes a score of three shots under par
Birdie	One under par
Bogey	One stroke over par. A bogey is a frightening mythical figure that golfers imagined themselves playing against when fixed scores for each hole were first introduced
Bunker	Sand dune
Caddie	The wee man or woman who carries the clubs and offers advice on the round
Fore!	Shouted out to warn other players of imminent danger from a mishit ball
Handicap	You can't play on a proper golf course without a handicap. This is the number over the course par (average) that it usually takes you to get round the course. This means that the worse you play, the higher your handicap and the more strokes you have to get round. Therefore if you play a better golfer, your skill levels are balanced, as he or she will have a lower handicap and therefore less strokes in which to get round the course in

Green fees	The amount you pay for a round of golf
Hole in one	Long distance fluke shot when the ball is holed with a single stroke
In the rough	When the ball is in the rough ground off the fairway
Irons	Golf clubs used to take medium-range shots. In the 19th century, each one had a name of its own and you would have had to choose between a *mid mashie*, *mashie niblick* or *cleek*
Links	A coastal course. Many famous golf courses in Scotland are links courses
The rub of the green	A common expression used to describe fickle weather conditions or bounces that make golf such an unpredictable and challenging sport
Spike bar	Bar in the clubhouse that you don't need to change from the course to enter
Spikes	Golfers shoes with spikes on them
Par	Meaning the 'usual or average', this is the standard set score in strokes for each hole
Parkland/ Highland courses	Inland settings for golf courses
Putter	The stick for the final moment(s) on the putting green

Scratch golfer	A golfer with a handicap of zero
Wood	Golf clubs with wooden bases used for long-range shots

SHINTY

Golf isn't Scotland's only homegrown sport. The sport of shinty, known as *camanachd* in Gaelic, is as old as Christianity's first awakenings in the Highlands. Introduced by Irish missionaries over two thousand years ago, the game has thrived ever since.

Shinty is a fast passing game with stick and ball between two teams over 90 minutes. Aiming for their opponents' goals, players hit a cork-filled leather ball in the air or on the ground. The game is fast and physical, looking like a cross between hockey, golf and Australian Rules football. There is one theory that the curved sticks, called *camans*, used by players inspired the invention of golf itself.

Shinty is most popular in and around the town of Newtonmore in the central Highlands. It's here that the Camanachd Association was founded in 1877, and where the yearly tussles with local rival Kingussie is played out for the Camanachd Cup.

THE HIGHLAND GAMES

Type 'The Highland Games' into an Internet search engine and references to it will pop up all over the world. It seems the game has travelled with homesick Highlanders to all the corners of the Earth. That's not surprising for a sport that is so quintessentially Scottish—a gritty trial of Herculean strengths with ball, hammer and *caber* (a tree trunk). Not to mention a piping competition that, according to one friend, "...puts to shame even the fiercest of catfights."

The oldest games didn't actually originate in the Highlands. Ceres in Fife first put on a show of strength in 1314 to celebrate the return of their 600 bowmen, triumphant from the battle of Bannockburn. The games nowadays are a mix of brawn, skill and dexterity. The main Herculean tests are throwing the hammer, tossing the *caber* and tug of wars. The lighter events are sprinting, fell running (running up hills), pole-vaulting and jumping. There is also room for invention— some days include anything from sheepdog trials and shinty to clay pigeon shooting or even pillow fighting.

The opening ceremony of a Highland games is a colourful pageant of dancing and piping. Highland dress is worn by many competitors—except of course, those competing in the pole vault. About 60 games are held across Scotland every year from July through September.

TOSSING THE COWPAT

Humour also plays its part in Scottish outdoor sports. A lesser known but no less bitterly contested competition is the national *cowpat* (manure) throwing competition. A suitably dry specimen is chosen for its weight and aerodynamics, and is thrown like a discus by young Adonises. The furthest throw wins the coveted trophy.

A friend still has his in a dusty cupboard from when he was crowned champion back in 1984. "The last man to throw got 108 feet," he recounted. "I stepped up and threw 113 feet, in fact I threw the *cowpat* so well it flew on past the perimeter and bounced off a car bonnet." Interviewed afterwards on national television, my friend put his big moment down to 'a lucky throw'.

SNOW LINES

From late October, snow starts dusting the mountaintops in the Highlands. By November, the downhill skiing season is in full swing, although the best snowfalls tend to come in January and February.

There are five ski centres in Scotland. These are the Nevis Range and Glencoe to the west and Glenshee, the Lecht and Cairngorm over to the east. In the winter, the village of Aviemore becomes something of a glamorous resort, with skiers enjoying Swiss chalet-style accommodation and easy access to the Cairngorm, the Lecht and Glenshee.

Skiing in these centres may not be as good, or as exotic, as the big resorts in continental Europe, but it is more affordable.

An average day pass is around £ 20 for adults and £ 10 for children. The centres also offer all-inclusive packages with five days board, skiing, hire and tuition costing as little as £ 150.00 per adult.

It's worthwhile checking the snow conditions on a daily basis before committing yourself to a day's skiing in Scotland. Conditions are unpredictable and you can find yourself enjoying pristine powder snow one day followed by a combination of rock, heather, slush and sheet ice the next. Scottish skiers tend to drive up to one of the centres for the day after a heavy snowfall.

DO YOU KEN?

CHAPTER 8

'Ah burrit Faither in the sand Mither opent the picnic
An made us a' piece an chicken roll—it wis braw'
—Opening stanza of 'The Beach' by Iain Harvey

THE SCOTS ARE GREAT COMMUNICATORS and it's hardly surprising that they have developed rich forms of expression. Not only does Scotland have its own dialect with a lot of regional variety in accents and expressions, it also maintains its own native language: Gaelic.

Being Scottish is closely tied up with the accent. Speak with a Scots accent and it doesn't really matter where you are originally from. So if you can pick up some of the local expressions and intonations, you will get that much warmer a reception. Scots is a beautiful and rich dialect that graces any foreign tongue well. I don't think I've heard a sweeter accent than from a Swedish girl who mixed up Irish, Swedish and Scots accents into a unique whole.

Note that not all Scots have Scots accents. There are those who grew up abroad and moved back but there are also true natives who don't have a Scots tinge. Most of these went to one of the country's private schools where the Queen's English is traditionally taught, rather than the local dialect.

GAELIC

Scotland's indigenous language isn't English, it's Gaelic. Gaelic is the language of the Celts and came from Ireland in the 6th century. Right up until the end of the 19th century, Gaelic was commonly spoken across much of Scotland. However, with the introduction of compulsory schooling in the 19th century, the language was actively discouraged and carried the stigma of being thought of as backwards and simple until relatively recently. In Ireland, Gaelic or Irish speakers used to be called 'bog hoppers'; rural types cut off from the modern world.

I remember as a boy hearing Gaelic spoken more than English by the old people on the west coast. Like a gentle rain, its soft lilt always fascinated me. Although we did have a few hours of Gaelic taught to us a week at school, for most of our generation, it was a case of too little too late. Gaelic spoken as a first language has been eroded back to the small islands like Harris and Lewis. The sense of its loss is still palpable to many, such as the poet Kenneth C Stephens who wrote:

'On Iona, the last Gaelic speaker has died...
...All over the Western Islands the last ones are going
like candles at night, falling across the wind
their last words lost and drowned in time.'

Gaelic may no longer be a commonly spoken language in Scotland, but it has enjoyed something of a revival in recent years. Gaelic speaker Paddy Shaw who lives outside the small village of Awe near Oban is encouraged by initiatives to keep the language alive. "There is a real resurgence going in the cities, with Gaelic medium schools, the Gaelic radio station *Radio nan Gaidheal* in Inverness and Gaelic television," Paddy told me. Much of the television is pitched toward children, who can now watch Gaelic versions of cartoons such as *Danger Mouse*, where the hero is renamed Donnie Murdo.

In Edinburgh, there are moves to make Gaelic part of the political lexicon. Some of the debates in Parliament are now being held in Gaelic. Although few on either side of the political divide speak fluent Gaelic, the initiative is an important recognition of what was Scotland's first language up until a couple of centuries ago.

Outside of the cities, there are also promising signs that Gaelic has a real future in Scotland. In the beautiful setting of Sleat in southern Skye, a Gaelic college has been running for some 30 years now. Called 'a big shed' or *Sabhal Mor*

Ostaig, the college is an important centre for anyone who wants to learn Gaelic, as well as being renowned for its late night sessions of folk music. There is also a Gaelic summer camp, called the Feis, for children on the islands of Tiree and Barra.

The biggest date in the calendar for Gaelic speakers is the Mod (the meeting). Organised by the Gaelic society, the Mod is a competitive festival of music, song, storytelling and dance that is held in early October in towns across Scotland. The Gaelic choirs are a high point at these festivals, which used to be a normal part of village life. Their strongholds are now in Argyll and the island of Barra.

There is hope for the survival of Gaelic as a living language. "More and more folk want to learn Gaelic and people like myself who speak the language are no longer looked down on, we are more envied or respected," said Paddy Shaw. But the survival of the language, so important to Scotland's cultural diversity, still hangs in the balance. "It's children that hold the future of the language. The problem is that when children become teenagers, they often loose interest and move away from the Gaelic scene," said Paddy.

SPEAK SCOTS

The Scots accent is one of the most distinctive in the English language, and according to most Sean Connery fans, one of the sexiest. However, Scots is much more than an accent. It's a dialect, rich in its own words and expressions.

A few hundred years ago, the English language in Scotland was so peppered with local expressions and phrases that 'Scots' was virtually a language in itself. Just read some of the 18th century poet Robert Burns' work and you will see how many of his words need translation. In school, students study 'Burns speak' to bring his poetry properly to life. There are several meticulously researched Scots dictionaries that cast light on many of the words that have since passed out of use.

There are still plenty of Scots phrases and expressions that can give an added dimension to speaking English in Scotland.

Whether it's saying '*aye*' instead of 'yes', '*wee*' instead of 'small' or '*tattie*' instead of 'potato', there is a host of new words even the most fluent of English speakers who visit or live in Scotland would have to learn.

Fifty years ago, there was an enormous amount of variety in accents and dialects across Scotland. Every area had a distinctive voice and set of colloquialisms. None more so than Glasgow that was so rich in local words and sayings that the dialect is known as 'the Glasgow patter'. With less people spending their whole lives in one village or valley, many of these regional distinctions have begun to be evened out.

But there are still big variations. For example, the accent on the west coast of the Highlands is softer and more singsong, reflecting the number of Gaelic speakers there for whom English was a second language in the past. Scots from rural Aberdeenshire in the Northeast have such a strong dialect that they can be particularly hard to follow. The accent from the lower Clyde is famous for its breakneck pace and bewildering mix of local expressions. The small islands can also have very distinctive accents. For example, people from Orkney (called Orcadians) have an unmistakable way of speaking. Their accents sound closer to Welsh than Scottish.

This sheer variety of accents may give each region of Scotland its own local colour, but it can be difficult to follow. Even if your first language is English, it can be a struggle to understand stronger dialects such as Glaswegian in full flow. There are no hard and fast pronunciation guidelines as Scots refuses to follow a neat format. Its richness is its diversity.

If you cannot keep up with the gist of the conversation, do not be afraid to ask for the phrase or sentence to be repeated; most Scots are patient and understanding with newcomers. If you are totally lost, just smile, nod your head and hope you aren't asked any direct questions. Of course, as in any new country, the longer you stay in Scotland, the more your ear will adjust to the patter.

HOT CONVERSATION TIPS

British people are masters at idle chit-chat and can while away hours saying nothing in particular. They tend to avoid talking about their real feelings, especially with strangers, so this kind of light conversation is a way of being friendly without being revealing. It is more noticeable south of the border where people tend to be more inhibited, but it is also relevant to Scotland, especially with the older generation.

Stepping into the social scene for the first time can be bewildering. Lucy Hunt, who moved to Scotland in the 1970s from Boston, first encountered the famous British reserve at a meal out with Scottish acquaintances. "They spent the first half hour talking about the weather," she said, "before rounding on price rises in the supermarket." Deciding that conversation needed a little bit of a boost, she attempted to move on to a passionate discussion about the political situation. The response was stunned silence—she had committed her first of many social faux pas.

In formal social environments or sit down dinners, religion, politics and sex are off the agenda. This is particularly true of the upper classes, where it is positively de rigueur to act a bit thick. Coming from an academic background where ideas and debate are valued, Lucy was often lost and somewhat bored. She has since learned the delicate art of small talk, filling silences by talking about things that are neither personal nor potentially contentious. "I feel I am just making a series of friendly noises, it's not what I would call a real conversation, but it does smooth the way," she says.

Younger Scots are much more vocal about what's on their mind. But when dining with strangers, it's safest to start with suitable general subjects such as the weather (in a maritime climate, there is always something to say!) and see where that takes you. It's hard to pin down what young people like to talk about, as they are generally happy to chat about anything once they get started. If you follow the football or the rugby, it can be a head start, particularly when chatting with men.

If that fails, recent films, what has been on television or what your plans are for the night or the weekend are also good conversation topics. Scots are generally more politicised than the English and are much informed and comfortable with discussions on the events of the day. They also tend to be more left wing in their outlook.

If all else fails, there is always that old gripe: the English. The Scots still love to complain about their poor treatment at the hands of their southern neighbours. Although there is perfectly good justification for this lingering bitterness, it's also true that it's easier to blame someone else for your troubles than deal with them yourself. The new Scots parliament and political devolution have brought with them a more positive attitude and now the negative talk about 'the English' is decreasing.

BODY LANGUAGE

Rebecca Castro, who moved to Scotland from Chile a year ago, is used to seeing more physical affection between friends. "I've made good friends here," she told me, "but I find it strange that the Scots aren't as touchy-feely as people are in warmer climes."

In Chile, no one escapes a 'hello' or 'goodbye' without a kiss on the cheek or a hug. In Scotland, a 'hello' or 'goodbye' comes with a handshake and often just a nod. Friends can say goodbye for a long parting and muster little more than a particularly rigorous handshake. Touching and kissing is generally restricted to sexual relations, particularly amongst older generations.

The space between two people speaking is also important. The British have a keen sense of personal space so it's best to keep your distance. If someone leans into your face while speaking to you in Scotland, it usually means that they either want to kiss you or are making a strong case for breaking both your arms.

Body language in Scotland is often contained. People don't swagger around unless drunk and seldom gesticulate with their hands. Likewise, the volume of conversations is lower than in countries like Chile or Italy. Step into a café in Scotland and you may notice that people tend to speak in muted toned compared to the Italians or Spanish, who seem to be constantly arguing to the British ear.

But this isn't the whole story. In a bar, much of this caution drops away. With an easy flow of drink, the Scots open up to friends and strangers alike. At a *ceilidh*, they are whirling dervishes, spinning and cantering around the dance floor with ease. But these are controlled environments where it's accepted to throw away inhibitions (with the odd drink). Social inhibitions are being worn away by new generations of Scots that travel and bring back more 'southern' and relaxed attitudes and customs to Scotland. Rebecca hopes that 'they will pass this more relaxed expression of feelings to their kids, and that the culture in Scotland will come to allow them a freer way to express themselves in public.'

DOING BUSINESS

CHAPTER 9

'Oh, it's nice to get up in the morning
And nicer to stay in bed.'
—Sir Harry Lauder,
Scottish music-hall comedian, singer and songwriter

THE ECONOMY

In the old days of the Industrial Revolution, doing business in Scotland was a relatively straightforward affair. The big industries—mainly shipping, cotton and jute—simply hammered and spun their wares for trade on the open seas.

Today, the Scotland of the big yards, looms and pits is remembered in albums of sepia photos for coffee tables. That isn't to say that the big industries are dead in Scotland; the yards on the north side of the Clyde still ring with the sound of construction. But labour-intensive industries have been in decline for a century, as the country increasingly adopts a service economy.

Many Scots still mourn the loss of some of the big industries, such as the Ravenscraig steel works in the 1980s, victims to the cold winds of free market economics and declining profits. Poverty and desperation brought on by higher unemployment has hit urban areas, such as Glasgow, hard. At football matches, Partick Thistle fans still sing 'You'll never work again' to rival fans from Motherwell, the area in Glasgow that supplied most of the labour to Ravenscraig.

The economy is now much more diverse, with many differing business interests working out of Scotland. For example, financial and business services now far exceeds engineering in employment. Edinburgh is an international centre for finance; the city ranks fourth after London, Paris and Frankfurt for international fund management.

The country's principal export is no longer iron or cotton, it is office machinery. The narrow strip of land between Glasgow and Edinburgh—known as Silicon Valley—produces over 30 per cent of branded personal computers in Europe. The electronics industry employs over 40,000 people in computer and software manufacture.

Of course, this isn't to say the advent of the brave new world of computers, international finance and the Internet marks the death knell of the old industries. Traditional businesses such as the fisheries, textiles, whisky, and more recently, oil and chemical manufacture, are still big sources of employment in Scotland's interdependent economy.

SOCIAL CUSTOMS AT WORK

Before even contemplating the likes of paying taxes or setting up shop in Scotland, you need to know your way around the social landscape. How to relate to people in the business culture without making a fool of yourself is essential. It is, after all, a rigid environment where simple cultural misunderstandings can break down working relationships into embarrassment or worse still, high farce.

Both dress sense and body language are sombre in business environments in Scotland. Suits and dark colours carry the day, even a flashy kipper tie to offset the sea of navy blue and grey is too showy. Introductions are equally formal. There is no physical contact beyond a round of handshakes and the odd pat on the back. It is important to look someone in the eye when you shake his or her hand and a good firm handshake is better respected than a limp one.

Whether meeting someone for the first or 100th time, they will probably ask you how you are. This is a greeting, more of a rhetorical question than a general inquiry into your well being. The answer is invariably "Fine, thanks," or "I'm OK, thanks." There is no need to give any more detail.

Business cards should be given out sparingly and never on the first introduction. You have to gain your potential

Don't kiss or hug someone unless you know him or her very well or are very drunk. An Italian friend once sealed a deal at a board meeting with a kiss on the senior partner's cheek. In the stunned silence that followed, he swore that his hair curled forever in embarrassment. In Scotland, men seldom kiss in public and certainly never at a business meeting.

business colleague's confidence with some small talk before steaming in with business cards and contact phone numbers. Cards are usually given out after you have found common ground, not before.

The business world in Scotland doesn't have the cosmopolitan and international feel of big urban centres such as London or New York. The social circles in Glasgow and especially Edinburgh are more restricted, making them harder to break into.

The old school network, meaning the friends and contacts made from university and school days, is not as strong as it was 20 years ago. But the logic still persists that most prefer to do business with people they know. Many connections and big jobs are shared amongst ex-university colleagues who meet in smoky clubs to drink fine whisky, share out power and generally think big.

Coming in from outside can be tricky to start with. For men, the old boys' clubs are nearly impossible to join unless you are nominated by one of the members. The best way to start meeting people is through sport. Golf is a popular meeting ground for businesses as you can both participate and talk shop. Remember that if you are playing golf, you'll need a good handicap to keep pace in the country that invented it.

For those who don't have the confidence, or the stamina, to streak around golf courses or football pitches, there are plenty of business forums, seminars and networking lunches organised by the likes of the Chamber of Commerce. The Small Business Gateway Service, part of the Scottish Enterprise Network, is also a good place to start meeting people. This government organisation has offices around Scotland and offers support to large and small businesses alike.

Scotland and Britain, in general, do not have the culture of the business lunch, so favoured in warmer, more laid-back countries. This doesn't mean that a three-hour boozy lunch is unheard of, but most settle for a sandwich in the office or a quick bite in a café.

A better bet for breaking the ice is a couple of drinks after work, although even this practice is surprisingly limited in Scotland. Apart from the ubiquitous few lost hours in the pub on a Friday evening, most scuttle home straight after work.

For women, the task of getting known and well connected is a little harder. An Australian businesswoman with years

Do's and Don'ts in the Workplace

Do's

- Do observe the dress code.
- Do be respectful of all your work colleagues, regardless of what position they hold.
- Do bring back a token present to the office from wherever you go on holiday.
- Do take time to socialise with work colleagues. It is expected and will make your job easier in the long run.
- Do go to the Christmas party as non attendance is frowned upon.

Don'ts

- Don't get blind drunk at the Christmas party.
- Don't smoke within the workplace.
- Don't tolerate any form of bullying or intimidation.
- Don't make sexist comments that could be misconstrued as harassment.
- Don't be late to appointments or meetings.
- Don't get involved in petty office politics unless you can not avoid it.
- Don't take long lunch breaks. Most workers stick to a quick sandwich at lunch unless they are entertaining a client.

of business experience in Scotland said, "Although the business culture is not overtly macho, the old boys clubs and the sporting side is a harder nut to crack if you're not one of the lads."

There are organisations, such as the East of Scotland Women's Club, that cater specifically to businesswomen, aiming to even up the balance a bit. But at the end of the day, women need just that little bit more guts to push themselves forward, especially in social situations.

The advantage of breaking into such a relatively small world in Scotland is that once your face is known—for better or for worse—the hard work is over. Make an impression on the social circuit and you're part of the crowd with your credibility (or lack of it) firmly established. Also, if you meet someone you think would make a valuable contact, you can be more or less assured that you will bump into them again. The same people inevitably come back round the merry-go-round of conferences and seminars.

Initially a little slow on the uptake in the Internet revolution, technological advances are now as much an aid to communication in Scotland as elsewhere in the business world. Most Scots have mobile phones and email addresses.

PARLEZ VOUS ANGLAIS?

Language barriers can present serious problems in Scotland. Although most big companies have access to translation facilities, almost all business is conducted in English. Few Scottish business people are competent in foreign languages—there is little need when English has become such a universal means of communication.

Even if you speak fluent English, coming to terms with the Scottish accent can still be a challenge. Vicky, an Australian friend, has lived and worked in Scotland for a year and still struggles at meetings to understand the accents of some of the senior personnel. "I have problems with Glaswegians and Aberdonians and telephone conversations can be very tricky," she told me.

STRESS

Stress is a buzzword in Britain. In fact, the word has virtually become a term for a medical condition in its own right, and covers a wide variety of symptoms. In London, a day doesn't pass when you hear someone complaining that they are 'sooo stressed out'. But then, working Londoners have to contend with long working hours, short lunches and high-pressured deadlines. At the end of each long day, they then have the pleasure of an average one-hour long commute home in a traffic jam or a sweaty underground train.

Scotland is a different story. The job market may not have the variety or the opportunities that London offers, but working conditions are generally much more civilised. Office hours tend to be what they are said to be—usually from 9:00 am to 5:30 pm. Cities in Scotland are also smaller and less congested, making commuting to work less time consuming.

The business culture tends to be more laid back than elsewhere. A good gauge of this is in the national attitude to time. In the office environment further south, every minute is precisely measured. If someone is late to work or to a meeting, it usually has to be for a very good reason.

In Scotland, time is more accurately measured out in coffee spoons than in minutes on the clock. Meetings usually start late and it's acceptable to turn up 5 or 10 minutes after the starting time. This more relaxed approach can be very frustrating if you are used to the business culture of countries such as Germany, which prides itself on good timekeeping.

Scotland may not have the same 110 per cent Protestant commitment to long working hours as in other countries, but times are changing. As the computer revolution pulls businesses into the same virtual world of global commerce, life at work is getting faster paced. Increased traffic on the roads and rocketing house prices also contribute to a picture of longer work hours and increasing stress levels.

JOB HUNTING

Badly paid jobs are easy to find in Scotland. Much of the young work force is employed in hotels, cafés, call centres and bars. Such jobs generally offer hard work, long hours and wages that are rarely above the national minimum wage of £ 5.73 an hour (for those 22 or over). Employees are often offered a few hours of part-time work a week, so that the employer is not obliged to give sick pay or other benefits.

Jobs such as these are advertised on the shop front window of the business, inviting people to apply within. They will expect to see your curriculum vitae (CV), the document listing your education, work experience and references. Lower paid jobs are also advertised at job centres. These government buildings, where unemployed people apply for state benefits, have hundreds of positions on offer, most of them unthinkable. You have to apply to them through one of the job centres' staff.

Recruitment or temping agencies also tender out work. This can be anything from silver service waiting at big functions to clerical work. The work offered can be on a permanent basis, or just a few weeks at a time. To find work with a temping agency, visit their offices in person with a

CV and references. You will be given a short interview to determine your suitability and availability.

Higher wage brackets and more permanent positions are harder to find. These sorts of positions are most commonly found advertised in *The Scotsman* and *The Herald* on Fridays. It would also be worthwhile sending in a CV and covering letter directly to the human resource department of the company that you are interested in, asking for work.

To apply to an advertised job, start by sending in a letter asking for further information and an application form. Complete this and send it back before the deadline indicated on the job advertisement. In most cases, you will be asked to include a CV and the addresses of two people willing to give references (known as referees).

If you are short-listed, you will be asked in a letter to attend an interview. If you don't get this far, you will usually receive a rejection letter. If you have an interview, phone first to confirm that you will be attending. Remember to dress formally on the day. A suit and tie for men and a smart dress or trousers for women is essential for most interviews. Some companies go on to ask for a second round of interviews or exhausting days of group assessment before a final decision is reached.

If you are chosen, you will usually be phoned and offered the job. Should you choose to ask for some time to think about it, or even turn it down, you are perfectly entitled to. Once you have accepted and signed a contract, you are committed.

Work for a Non Governmental Organisation (NGO)

Scotland has a burgeoning Non Governmental sector which is becoming increasingly attractive to young professionals. Working conditions are often more flexible and there can be real job satisfaction in committing yourself to a good cause. The disadvantage is in pay—expect to get considerably less that you would in the business world.

Competition for paid positions in Non Governmental Organisations is fierce. Many find that volunteering is a good first step to see if the work suits them, and in some cases, to help get a foot in the door. There are no shortage of volunteering opportunities in Scotland, from social work, to tree planting to whale and dolphin watching. For further information and the latest vacancies, check out the Scottish Council for Voluntary Organisations website at http://www.scvo.org.uk.

BUSINESS IN SCOTLAND

The first step towards understanding how companies operate or set up shop in Scotland is to understand the different business forms. There are three main types:

Sole Trader

This is the easiest and quickest way to get started. You alone are responsible for the business, so you can either get rich quick or end up personally liable for a mountain of debt.

The advantages of a sole trader over other forms of business entities are that the paperwork is minimal, accounts are kept confidential and there is greater flexibility on tax payment. Converting a business into a limited company is also a relatively easy process, although transferring the ownership to another sole trader can be a bureaucratic headache.

Partnership

In a partnership, two or more people arrange to share the responsibilities for the joint running of a business. The partners are jointly and severally responsible for any debts incurred by the business. This means that if one partner fails to cover his or her financial commitments, the other party or parties have to make up the shortfall.

The added risk is human. Partnerships, generally set up between friends, can end up being dissolved by bitter and impoverished enemies. It is therefore vital to draw up an agreement that clearly lays out each party's responsibilities to help avoid possible conflicts.

Limited Company

A limited company has a life of its own. It is a separate legal entity with directors and shareholders. Its main features are:

- The company is liable for its business debt, so shareholders can only lose the money they initially spent to buy shares. However, a lender may still ask for personal guarantees from directors, such as their house, as security on a loan.
- It is easier to spread out or pass on the ownership of a limited company and is therefore ideal for someone who wants to invest with shares without getting involved in day-to-day management.
- Income tax is only paid on salaries and perks. However, National Insurance contributions are much higher for limited companies than they are for other business entities.
- A limited company has more credibility in the business world as records and accounts are obliged to be kept at Company's House for anyone to inspect should they wish to.

Co-operative and Community Businesses

Cooperatives are surprisingly popular in Scotland, and can be anything from building societies to bicycle shops. In a co-operative, the employees own the business equally and share in its running profits and losses.

A variation on the same idea is a community business, owned by a group of people with the same interests who live in the same area. A good example of this is the community buyout of the island of Eigg on Scotland's west coast in 1997. Fed up with a series of absentee landlords, the local inhabitants formed the Isle of Eigg trust and, with the help of the Scottish Wildlife Trust and the Highland Council, bought the island to manage themselves.

EMPLOYEES' RIGHTS

The numerous acts of parliament, as well as European regulations concerning employment in Scotland, makes it a complex area to understand. With Britain's ongoing integration into the European Union, there are also bound to be more changes in coming years. For detailed and up-to-date information, it is best to contact the local Benefits Agency office or Citizens Advice Bureau.

Employment conditions in Scotland vary widely. Unless you are employed for less than one month, you are entitled by law to have your conditions of employment set out in a written statement, including the basics such as hours, holiday entitlement and pay. The following basic working rights apply to all employees:

- According to European Law, an employee cannot be forced to work for more than 48 hours in a week. However, an employee can work longer hours if he or she chooses to. This is agreed in a written statement with the employer that can be cancelled by the employee at any time in writing.

- Employees are legally entitled to join and take part in the activities of a trade union.

- The National Minimum Wage Act 1998 introduced a legal minimum hourly rate that must be paid to everyone 18 years old or over. The current rate is £ 5.73 for those 22 or over.

- Employers are obliged to provide sick pay to workers who are off due to illness. However, the length of time and amount of money an employee is covered varies with each employer. The law concerning statutory sick pay is complex and open to interpretation. 'Throwing a sickie', or taking a day off from work with an invented ailment is a national pastime in Britain. These days, wary employers often ask for doctor's notes as proof that their sick employee is genuinely bedridden.

- If an employee is dismissed, he or she is entitled to a written statement giving the reasons for dismissal within 14 days. If an employee feels unfairly dismissed and has worked for 52 weeks or more, he or she can seek compensation in a tribunal. Claims must be made within three months, so it is important that you act quickly. Free legal representation, known as 'legal aid', is not available at employment tribunal hearings. However, 'legal advice and assistance' is. The Citizens Advice Bureau is the first port of call if you need to go down this road.

Maternity Leave

Maternity leave is yet another minefield of complex legislation. What is certain is that no woman can be dismissed on grounds of pregnancy or childbirth. If the pregnancy makes it impossible for the employee to carry out her duties, she can be suspended on full pay or assigned to another position within the company until after the child is born.

Pregnant employees are also entitled to time off work for antenatal care as well as paid maternity leave before and after the child is born. Provided the employee gives at least 21 days' notice (in writing) of her planned absence, her job must remain open for her to return to after her maternity leave.

It is illegal for an employer to allow a woman to return to work within the first two weeks of her giving birth and all women have the right to a basic 18 week maternity leave period. If the employee has been with the company for more than one year's continuous employment, she is entitled to an extended 29 weeks of leave, now called 'additional maternity leave'.

Paternity Leave

Fathers are finally being recognised in the law for their role in childcare. Any new dad who has been in continuous employment for at least one year is now entitled to two weeks paid paternity leave and at least 13 weeks of unpaid paternity leave.

Fair Play

Women are by law entitled to the same pay as men for work of the same value. Under the Equal Pay Act of 1970, if there is a salary difference offered by an employer for the same job, it has to be justified by reasons other than gender. It is also unlawful to discriminate against women, or men for that matter, in the workplace. Due to European directives, this now includes the practice of positive discrimination, or deliberately employing either men or women to make up a better gender balance.

On an island that is increasingly becoming a melting pot of different peoples, there is sound legislation in place to protect Scotland's ethnic minorities in the workplace. Under the Race Relations Act 1976, it is unlawful to discriminate against a person on grounds of colour, race, nationality or ethnic origins.

The Commission for Racial Equality—set up to give the above law teeth—helps employees who feel that they have been wronged for racial reasons. The Race Relations Act covers all forms of employment, with the exception of work done in private households and work which would naturally require a person of a certain nationality or ethnic origin (such as Russian Cossack dancing).

THE TAX MAN

Resented across the land, the taxman is never far from any earnings or business ventures. The offices of the Inland Revenue produce lots of cheap and cheerful literature with smiling people explaining how fun it is to pay taxes. They don't fool anyone. The Inland Revenue is a labyrinth of departments, forms are complex and difficult to decipher and there are heavy punishments if you are caught on the dodge. The following is a cursory glance of what lies in store for the potential employer or employee.

National Insurance

Whether you are an employer, employee or self-employed, you have to pay National Insurance and income tax towards your State Retirement Pension and other Social Security benefits. The amount due for National Insurance depends on how successful the business is, or your salary. There are several ways to pay National Insurance. Contact the local Department of Social Security office to negotiate which is best suited to you.

Pay As You Earn

If you employ someone, including yourself, you become your own tax collector under the Pay as you Earn (PAYE) system. You are responsible for assessing and deducting income tax

Guards in traditional dress offer a colourful welcome to the Edinburgh Castle.

St Andrew's Cathedral, the main church of the
Archdiocese of Glasgow and the focal point
for the Roman Catholic population in Glasgow.

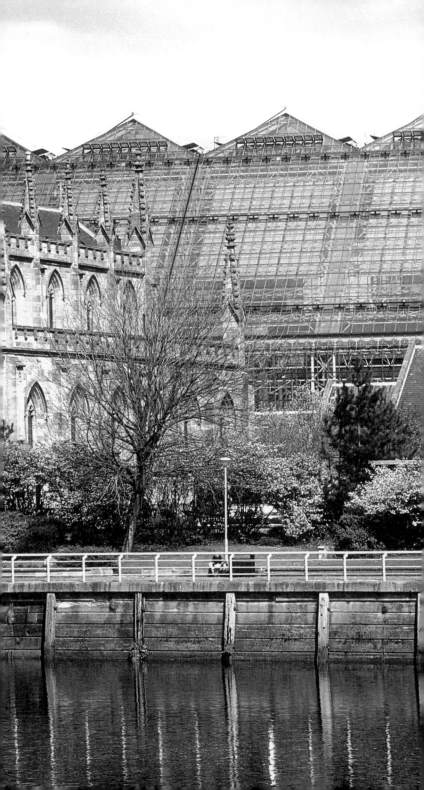

Musical entertainment at the Edinburgh Festival.
Right: Advertisements for the three-week
festival, which boasts outstanding performances
of all kinds and visitors from all over the world.

Golf is hugely popular in Scotland.

Deacon Brodie's Tavern, a well-known watering hole in Edinburgh.

and National Insurance from your own or your employee's earnings. This money is then deducted from an employee's net pay and sent to the Inland Revenue. On leaving a job, you are entitled to claim back the tax that has been deducted if you have been on a low wage.

Value Added Tax

Value Added Tax (VAT), currently 15 per cent, is charged on most business transactions in the UK. VAT is charged on all goods and some services that are imported into the country.

VAT is not levied on everything. Some of the exceptions are professional training, some types of insurance, non-luxury foods, newspapers, books, children's clothing and new houses. Your local VAT office—in the telephone directory under Customs and Excise—can give up-to-date information on VAT's long-armed reach.

Where relevant, VAT is charged by most suppliers. However, only companies that trade over a prescribed amount have to register for VAT payment. Being VAT registered means that you are obliged to invoice your customers for an additional 15 per cent of the original charge. A company whose turnover exceeds the minimum amount but doesn't register may have to pay for the VAT it did not charge its customers.

An accountant is a great help when it comes to disentangling yourself from the VAT maze. Accountants give advice, help make claims to all allowances due and make sure that records are accurately maintained.

Income Tax for a Sole Trader or Partnership

The tax year for income tax runs from 6 April to 5 April. Sole traders and partnerships have to pay income tax on their annual profits, as shown in their annual accounts. They are expected to pay this tax in two instalments, on 31 January and 31 July.

The Inland Revenue now operates a system of self-assessment. This means that you can calculate the taxes that you owe yourself, or you can ask the Inland Revenue to calculate it on your behalf. If a company makes a loss over the first four years of business, it may be able to recover some of the income tax that it has paid out.

Corporate Tax for a Limited Company

As a limited company, you will be paying income taxes on wages to yourself—and any other employees—under the PAYE scheme mentioned above.

In addition to income tax, limited companies have to pay corporate tax on their profits. The rate of tax for companies with profits below £ 30,000 is currently 21 per cent. Britain's corporate tax is 28 per cent for companies that generate more than £ 30,000 of profit. If a company has previously been running at a loss, it can set its profits against the previous three years losses, or carry them forward for future tax returns.

SETTING UP YOUR OWN BUSINESS

Nicolas Stepanopolus knows the ups and downs of setting up a small business first-hand. He came over to Scotland from his home country of Greece in 1997, fell in love with a local girl and settled down.

Hating the idea of working for someone else, Nicolas decided to set up a café in Edinburgh with his Scottish friend Graham, selling fresh organic juices and Mediterranean food. The café, called Lianachan, after the Gaelic word for *wee meadow*, is a bright and simple place with high ceilings and wooden tables. Nicolas sits by a window seat flooded with light that catches the lazy curl of his cigarette smoke.

Taking in the peaceful scene, you would never guess just how fraught the process of setting up the café has been. It has not been an easy road, bringing that first idea to life in brick, mortar and frothy cappuccinos. The truth is that for both Nicolas and Graham, setting up their own business has been an exhausting and at times bewildering journey. Nicolas looks like he's blinking away the darkness after finally slaying the Minotaur and tracing the string back out of the maze—of paperwork.

Nicolas outside the Lianachan café.

"It was very, very frustrating to organise all of these things; getting properly set up, signing all of these papers and all the money, money, money that disappears to all these people," he explains.

To set up a business in Scotland, you need money, patience and a lot of ink. There is a whole host of expenses, legal requirements and forms to be filled with financial penalties for those who don't comply.

The Paper Chase

The problems start as soon as you decide on a name for your new business. Trading under your own name, or names if the business is a partnership, is relatively straightforward. However, life can get complicated if you decide to trade under a separate business name.

Names that suggest a connection with the government, or which may be deemed offensive are non-starters. For example, the FART Bus Company in Spain would quickly offend the British sense of decency! Company's House has the complete list of trade names in use and can advise on any restricted words and phrases.

Then you have to let your local tax office know as soon as you start trading. The address is in the local telephone directory under 'Inland Revenue'. You also have to contact the local department of Social Security, who coordinates the payment of National Insurance.

You may also have to register to pay Value Added Tax although this depends on the business. Contact your local Value Added Tax Office, listed under 'Customs and Excise' in the telephone directory, to find out if you do.

Limited companies have to be registered with the Companies House. They need to come up with the names of at least one shareholder, director and company secretary, details of the share capital, a Memorandum of Association and an Article of Association.

There are a host of other legal requirements in setting up a business. You may need a licence to carry out business activity from your local council or from national government departments such as the Department of Environment. This can apply to anything from pubs, hairdressers, dog breeders to sex shops. Nicolas' and Graham's café needed licences from the Department of Environmental Health to play music and prepare food. Selling alcohol and staying open late required separate licences.

It's best to contact a local Business Development Centre for advice on what applies to you. With all of Britain coming into line with European Union regulations, the rules and regulations are often being updated and reviewed.

If you are importing goods, you'll need to contact the Department of Trade and Industry to get a licence and pay the relevant taxes. However, it is worth asking your local Customs and Excise office for the tariff numbers of the goods you wish to import. Goods from the European Union come licence free and often without import tariffs.

Financing the Slippery Pole

Anyone who has set up a business knows how much initial investment is needed to get it up and running. That first lump sum of equity capital—usually twice as much as you initially expect—can make or break businesses as they struggle to get off the ground. There are all kinds of sources for funding in Scotland, and most businesses draw on some combination of all of them.

Private Funding

Private funding is the obvious and most straightforward of options. This can be your own money and/or help from family and friends. The general rule is that if you can't put up around 30 per cent of the start-up capital yourself, the banks won't show much interest in making up the shortfall.

Bigger businesses can also look for more formal help from Venture Capitalists, also known as 'business angels'. These 'equity' investors look for their return in a share of the business profits and a cut of any sale. The money they give—generally over £ 300,000—is not expected to be repaid like a bank loan. With such large sums involved, 'business angels' will seldom look at anything other than established businesses with high profit turnovers that are looking to expand. If they do get involved, they can bring with them a lot of kudos and expertise but they also expect have a significant say in how the business is run.

Public Sector

A softer option than fat cat 'business angels' for new businesses is public sector funding. Government grants are generally more readily available in Scotland than in other European countries. Most sources of funding stress that the money must be used to fill in financial shortfalls instead of funding business start-up costs.

Big grants are more likely to go to employers who can promise work for more than 20 people. Manufacturing and high technology are the most favoured with retail and personal services raising little interest. The most important contact for grants between £ 50,000 and £ 500,000 is the Scottish Equity Partnership. Set up in 1996, the Partnership funds new and growing businesses. Several other grants are available for smaller businesses. However, these are often only advertised locally and are difficult to find. A good place to start looking is the Local Business Shop, a government information body offering information and advice on all business matters free of charge.

Nicolas is very grateful for the support that he got from the Edinburgh Small Business Gateway Service after deciding to set up his business. They helped him with an intensive course in how to set up and run a new business venture, follow-up support and a small amount of cash to help get by in lean times.

"If we didn't have them, we'd be lost in space," said Nicolas. "And they come free," he added.

Bank Loans

Banks generally provide no more than 40 per cent of the financing for a new business venture. How successful you are with the bank depends on a number of factors. Most important is the quality of your business plan, the prospects for generating revenue over the medium term and security for the bank.

'Security' is their guarantee that if it all goes pear-shaped and you have to close down, they can still get their original investment back. In other words, you may end up signing over your house as security for a loan.

Finding Business Premises

Buying a home is complicated enough in Scotland. There's an entirely new set of regulations that need consideration when buying or leasing a business property or running a business from home.

If you decide on setting up at home, then beware. The title deeds or lease of the property have to be free of restrictions as some prohibit business use on the premises. You also have to get the OK from the local Environmental Health Departments to check that you meet health and fire regulations. For example, if catering is involved, you will probably be required to have a separate kitchen, even if all you're making is tea and coffee.

You will also need to contact the planning department of the local council. If the business will mean an increase in traffic or noise, there is a good chance that complaining neighbours will force you to close shop. It's also a good idea to be sure that house insurance also covers business equipment, as many insurance companies are reluctant to take on the added risk.

If you are renting or buying a commercial property, the same system applies with finding a home. The best place to start looking is in the property pages of national and local newspapers. It's also worth being put on the mailing list of local solicitors, developers, surveyors and estate agents as they also lease out and sell commercial property in Scotland. For small workshops or short-term rental, try Railtrack property (railway arches are a cheap way to start up), British Steel PLC and industrial estates found around most small towns.

The whole process can take a long time and be very expensive. Finding the right place for Nicolas' café took over a year. "We were looking for months, tramping the streets and wearing out our sandal leather," he said.

A small space of prime real estate in the centre of town didn't come cheap either. After forking out £ 4,500 worth of deposit money, Nicholas is committed to paying £ 2,500 every three months in rent for the next six years.

Get Yourself Connected

There are about 20 million new users logging onto the Internet every month. It's nothing short of a revolution in how we access and distribute information.

The business world has been quick on the uptake, recognising that e-commerce jumps the barriers of geography, time and culture. You can buy almost anything online, from a pork pie to a private island. Many small start-up companies in Britain are making millions on the Internet, although the market is still volatile with fortunes made and lost in the blink of the stock market's eye.

Nowadays, technology means that most businesses can be run from home, all that is needed is a telephone, fax machine and computer. This means that it is now possible for a person to live in a lovely Highland glen and still have his or her finger on the pulse of their business venture. Mobile phones and email have made communication with the central workplace effortless. Buying the equipment is a simple affair. Office equipment, especially computers, is readily available from high street stores. Often the best deals can be found online, or in computer magazines, available at most newsagents. Just make sure if you get one of these bargains that the guarantee is a good one.

Businesses are now quick to get a presence on the Internet with their own web page. There are a plethora of design companies that will charge anything from a few hundred to thousands of pounds to put you on the net. Alternatively, designing your own page is relatively simple if you have the relevant software, some courage and a little IT know-how. It's worth remembering that with approximately one website for every three people on the planet, designing your website so that it pops up on the main search engines is as important as having a site with all the bells and whistles.

Insurance

Getting the right insurance to cover potential disasters is essential in any business. There are a large number of insurance policies available that will cover premises, goods and most eventualities.

If you employ people, you are obliged by law to take out employer's liability insurance. This protects you from accident or illness claims made by your employees. You can also get insurance to cover potential claims arising from faults in your products or from professional negligence.

If you need a vehicle for work, it also needs business insurance. It's important to check that the insurance policy covers you and any employee using the vehicle for commercial activities.

It's best to shop around. You can either go straight to insurance companies or to an insurance broker; both are listed in the *Yellow Pages*. For the cost of a phone call and a small fee, insurance brokers will shop around the market for the cheapest quote and arrange for the relevant cover on your behalf.

Keeping Accounts

New companies, especially limited companies, generate mountains of paperwork. All invoices, receipts and other papers should be kept on file, as it is necessary to have proof of all business transactions for the Inland Revenue or VAT inspectors. Accounts can and probably will be assessed by the Inland Revenue so it is important to be meticulous with bookkeeping.

Nicolas does his own accounts at Lianachan, a daily chore that involves logging in everything that he pays in and out of the business account. "This is for tax purposes," he tells me as he works on a sheet of finely scrawled figures. "But it is also useful for forecasts and budgeting." At the end of the financial year in April, his accountant tidies up and reviews the year's progress. A bigger business can, of course, afford to hand over everything to the accountant.

Either way, professional help from a lawyer or an accountant is essential, even if you can't afford the high fees. Lawyers are useful for drawing up a good business plan, applying for licences or for handling legal wrangles. Accountants help with annual accounts, Value Added Tax returns and other financial matters.

It is important to estimate how much you are likely to have to pay and keep back enough money for the taxes when they are due. In Britain, up to a year and a half can pass before a first demand is made for payment of a tax bill.

Survival

Back at the café, Nicolas eases back into his chair and looks out of the window with a weary smile. Although he's survived the process of setting up his own business, the stress and hard work is still far from over. He has to worry about advertising the café, cooking up novel and tasty dishes and paying the rent in a month's time.

But for the moment, he remembers the rewards of going into it alone with a little help from his friends. "Being self-employed, that's what it is all about. It's worth it, it's an adventure. There's a lot of stress but we'll see it work out."

'The rose of all the world is not for me.
I want for my part
Only the little white rose of Scotland
That smells sharp and sweet—and breaks the heart.'
—Hugh MacDiarmid (1892–1978),
Scottish poet and nationalist

Official Name
Scotland

Capital
Edinburgh

Flag
Light blue background with a white X-shaped cross going across its diagonals from corner to corner. This is known as the Saint Andrew's cross

National Anthem
Flower of Scotland

Time
Greenwich Mean Time plus + 1 hour (GMT + 0100)

Telephone Country Code
44

Land
Scotland and its offshore islands comprise the northernmost part of the United Kingdom. The Scottish mainland, which occupies roughly the northern third of the island of Great Britain, is bordered on three sides by seas. To the north and west is the Atlantic Ocean; to the east is the North

Sea. Rugged uplands separate Scotland from England to the south

Area
78,783 sq km (30,418 sq miles)

Highest Point
Ben Nevis (1,343 m / 4,406 ft)

Climate
Temperate winters and cool summers

Natural Resources
Oil, hydroelectric power, coal, iron, wind

Population
5,078,400 (June 2004)

Ethnic Groups
Celtic Scots, Anglo-Saxons, Scandinavians, Lithuanians, Italians, Poles and Pakistanis

Religion
Church of Scotland (Presbyterianism denomination), Roman Catholicism

Official Language
English

Government Structure
Scotland has its own devolved parliament in Edinburgh, the Scottish Executive, as well as political representation in Westminster, London

Adminstrative Divisions
32 council areas: Aberdeen City, Aberdeenshire, Angus, Argyll and Bute, Scottish Borders, Clackmannanshire, Dumfries and Galloway, Dundee City, East Ayrshire, East Dunbartonshire,

East Lothian, East Renfrewshire, City of Edinburgh, Falkirk, Fife, Glasgow City, Highland, Inverclyde, Midlothian, Moray, North Ayrshire, North Lanarkshire, Orkney Islands, Perth and Kinross, Renfrewshire, Shetland Islands, South Ayrshire, South Lanarkshire, Stirling, West Dunbartonshire, Eilean Siar (Western Isles) and West Lothian

Currency
Sterling pound (£)

Gross Domestic Product (GDP)
£ 86.3 billion (2006)

Agricultural Products
Wheat, oats, and potatoes. Other crops include barley, turnips and fruit

Industries
Electronics, manufacturing, oil and natural gas, textiles, whisky production

Exports
Manufactured goods, fuels, chemicals, food, beverages, tobacco, whisky

Imports
Manufactured goods, machinery, fuels, foodstuffs

Airports
489. The main international airports are at Glasgow and Edinburgh. Scotland's other main airports are at Preswick, Aberdeen, Inverness and Dundee.

FAMOUS PEOPLE
Here are some of the most important names to remember while you're in Scotland. Know a little about them and you can bluff your way through most high- or low-brow conversations.

Saint Columba (521–597)

6th century Celtic firebrand who brought Christianity to the Pictish people and was buried on Iona.

Macbeth (unknown–1057)

King of Scots from 1040 who fought off the English only to be immortalised as evil incarnate in Shakespeare's play of the same name.

Sir William Wallace (1270–1305)

Patriot, national hero and chief defender of Scotland's independence in the 13th century.

Robert the Bruce/Robert VIII de Bruce (1274–1329)

Actually an Anglo-Norman, Robert the Bruce tenaciously defeated English forces at the Battle of Bannockburn in 1314, ushering in a long period of independence for the fledgling Scottish nation.

Mary Queen of Scots (1542–1587)

Stuart queen whose tumultuous life, ending with her beheading at the order of Queen Elizabeth I, has something of the love, tragedy and fury of the country she has become a symbol for.

John Knox (1514–1572)

Protestant reformer and bitter enemy of the Catholic Mary Queen of Scots. Wrote *The History of the Reformation in Scotland*.

King James VI (1566–1625)

The first king of both England and Scotland, who styled himself 'King of Great Britain'.

Bonnie Prince Charlie (1720–1788)

The Young Pretender. Made an audacious bid for the British throne with the Highlander's support in 1745, only to be defeated at the Battle of Culloden.

Flora MacDonald (1722–1790)

Scottish Jacobite heroine who helped Bonnie Prince Charlie flee the English after the Battle of Culloden. She has been immortalised in folk tales and songs ever since.

Robert (Rob Roy) MacGregor (1671–1734)

Swashbuckling cattle thief who recently hit the big time in the film *Rob Roy*.

James Boswell (1740–1795)

Boswell was a biographer and traveller and is best known for his description of his journeys with Sir Samuel Johnson to the Scottish highlands and islands.

Robert (Robbie) Burns (1759–1796)

Scotland's best-known poet and songwriter, whose words were almost as prolific as his womanising.

Sir Walter Scott (1771–1832)

Practised as a lawyer but famed as a poet and novelist. Best known are the Waverly novels, which include *Rob Roy*, *Ivanhoe* and *The Heart of Midlothian*.

Thomas Carlyle (1795–1881)

Historian and essayist who wrote on such epic themes as the French Revolution and Fredrick the Great.

David Livingstone (1813–1873)

The most famous of the wandering Scots. 19th century explorer who took on one inhospitable jungle too many, and also discovered Victoria falls.

Sir Arthur Conan Doyle (1859–1930)

Author and creator of the worlds most famous detective, Sherlock Holmes.

John Muir (1838–1914)

Considered the father of the modern environmental movement for saving Yosemite Park from lumber men in

California's Sierra Nevada. The John Muir Trust was formed in 1985 to acquire and conserve wild land in Britain.

Robert Louis Stevenson (1850–1844)

Author or such much loved classics such as *Kidnapped* and *Treasure Island*. Died living the life of his fictional adventurers on the island of Samoa.

The Big Inventors

Scotland is famed for its inventive streak, particularly in medicine. To name a few, John Williamson found a vaccine for small pox, James Lind cured scurvy with lemons, Ronald Ross traced malaria to mosquitoes and Sir James Young Simpson discovered that chloroform is a great anaesthetic.

The Scots have been responsible for some big advances in modern technology. We must thank Alexander Bell for the telephone, John Logie Baird for pioneering the television, James Watt for inventing the steam engine and Sir James Dewar for coming up with the humble thermos flask. In 1996, scientists in the Roslin Institute outside of Edinburgh successfully cloned the first animal, Dolly the sheep.

MODERN DAY CELEBRITIES

Robert Carlyle

Highly acclaimed actor who made his mark in the film *Trainspotting*, as well as playing lead roles in *Riff Raff*, *Carla's Song* and *The Full Monty*.

Ewan MacGregor

Actor who first found fame playing drug addict Renton in the film version of Irvine Walsh's *Trainspotting*. Has since become a Hollywood star, author and UN ambassador.

Sean Connery

007 agent with a licence to kill and break hearts. Ever popular with the ladies, he has appeared in plenty of films since his James Bond days but has never quite shrugged off the 'shaken, not stirred' image.

Billy Connolly

Arguably Scotland's finest comedian. With a rich career on the stage and the big screen behind him, 'The Big Yin' has come a long way since his *Great Northern Welly Boot Show* in the Edinburgh festival in the early seventies. He now lives in America.

Sir Alex Ferguson

Highly respected manager of Manchester United football club.

Annie Lennox

Pop diva from Aberdeen who, together with Dave Stewart, did much to lighten up a decade of outlandish hairstyles and crashing music.

Charles Rennie Mackintosh

Glasgow artist, architect and designer who is enjoying fresh fame for his stylish designs.

Shirley Manson

Edinburgh girl made good in the music world. Headed the bands Goodbye Mr Mackenzie and Garbage. Now based in America.

Ally McCoist

Called 'Super Ally' by his fans, McCoist is famous for being a superb striker for Rangers and an all round nice guy. Now makes regular appearances on TV.

Joe McFadden

Long standing actor in Scottish drama *Take the High Road*, also principle actor in TV adaptation of Ian Banks best-selling novel *The Crow Road*.

Andy Murray

Scottish tennis sensation who has fought his way up the ranks to become one of the worlds highest ranking players. Murray was runner up in the 2008 US Open and is currently Britain's best chance of winning the men's singles at Wimbeldon.

Eduardo Paolozzi
Edinburgh-based painter and sculptor of Italian descent who in recent years has become a household name.

Sir Jackie Stewart
Formula One world champion in 1969, 1971 and 1973. David Coulthard is the latest Scottish speed demon to grace the Formula One tracks.

Taggart
Dour Glaswegian police inspector of the long-standing series of the same name who is far tougher than the villains he tracks down. Most likely to say, "There's bin a murdur."

Robbie Coltrane
Actor and comedian, best recognised in the comic films *Nuns on the Run* and *The Pope Must Die*. Most recently seen on television in the dark detective series *Cracker* and as Hagrid in the *Harry Potter* movie series.

ACRONYMS IN POLITICS
Green	Green Party
Lab	Labour Party
MSP	Minister of the Scottish Parliament
SNP	Scottish National Party
SWP	Scottish Workers' Party

PLACES OF INTEREST
Scotland is dotted with 1,001 places of interest so these are just a few of my personal favorites. They may not be the most obvious or the most popular places on the tourist map, but they all leave the visitor a little more enchanted with the country and people. Find out more about people's favourite haunts in Scotland at http://placebookscotland.com.

Arthur's Seat, Edinburgh
No visit to the capital is complete without scaling Arthur's seat, a rocky crag in heart of the city. From here, you have a

panorama that take in the Firth of Forth, Edinburgh University and the Pentland Hills.

Museum of Scotland, Edinburgh
An eclectic introduction to Scotland's history. Make sure you visit the restaurant on the top floor for superb views and great food.

Gallery of Modern Art, Glasgow
Scotland's finest artists, many of them painters, are on show in this classy gallery in the city centre.

New Lanark, South Lanarkshire
A restored cotton mill village and world heritage site, New Lanark gives a fascinating flavour of everyday life during the industrial revolution.

Melrose Abbey, Melrose, The Borders
Scotland's most spectacular ruin, Melrose Abbey is a tour though centuries of architectural design, conflict and decay. It is also home to the heart of Scotland's hero king Robert the Bruce.

Shores of Loch Lomond
The bonnie banks of Loch Lomond have been celebrated in song and poetry for centuries. It may not be the most original of destinations but it is still hard to beat for beauty and romance. It is also now the gateway for the newly created Loch Lomond and Trussocks National Park.

Tantallon Castle, Berwick, Lothian
There are plenty of better known castles in Scotland but few have the setting of Tantallon Castle. Perched on the sea's edge, it looks towards the bird sanctuary Bass Rock and is reputed by some to be the castle of King Arthur's Camelot.

Scottish Fisheries Museum, Anstruther, Fife
Loose yourself in this journey back to the days when the herring fishery dominated the work, lives and customs of

the east coast of Scotland. Step across the street and wash the experience down with the finest fish and chips in the kingdom of Fife.

Glen Lyon, Perthshire

Known as the longest, loveliest and loneliest glen in Scotland, there are few places in the world that come as close to Narnia as Glen Lyon.

Glen Affric, Inverness-shire

Glen Affric is the home to one of the largest ancient Caledonian pine forests in Scotland. This is how the landscape looked before these forests were felled centuries ago. The area has recently been designated a national nature reserve.

Scara Brae, Orkney

Orkney is home to numerous archeological remains including stone circles and Viking settlements. But nothing beats a visit to recently discovered Scara Brae, an entire Neolithic village on the sea, complete with stone beds, shelves and dressers that rival many modern designs.

Beaches of Harris, Harris

The Bermuda of northern Europe, the island of Harris in the Outer Hebrides has bone white beaches and turquoise seas that rival any Caribbean hot spot. That is until you decide to go for a swim.

CULTURE QUIZ

SITUATION 1

You mistakenly ask a Scotsman or woman where they come from in England. Do you:

Ⓐ Apologise profusely.
Ⓑ Beg for forgiveness.
Ⓒ Change the subject and hope they didn't hear the question.

Comments

None of the above, as you will be curtly corrected before you can get in a response. The Scots may now have their own parliament and with it a greater sense of self-confidence and separation from England, but they are still touchy when it comes to being confused with the English.

Canadians are so used to being mistaken with Americans when they are abroad that they tend to accept being confused with their Southern neighbours with a mix of grace and weary resignation. The Scots are not so forgiving. It is still common in Scotland to hear 'The English' lumped together and derided as being arrogant, insensitive and just about everything else under the sun. So mistakenly calling someone from Scotland English is not a wise move.

Although an English or Scots accent is a pretty reliable marker of identity, it is far from foolproof. There are plenty of well-to-do Scots who lost their accents in private schools in England. And then there are all the immigrants and expatriates who have come back from abroad that further confuse the picture. If in doubt, it is best to assume that everyone in Scotland is Scottish regardless of their accent and wait to see if you are told otherwise. An even worse slip up is to refer to the islands of Great Britain as England. This is enough to make the blood of anyone from Scotland, Wales or Ireland boil.

SITUATION 2

You and a friend have gone camping on the west coast of Scotland. It is mid-July and you have walked the long daylight hours until dusk before hurriedly throwing up the tent in the gathering night. You wake up the following morning (your head still brimming from an evening under the stars by the campfire) to the now familiar sound of fine rain on the tent roof. You poke your head out of the tent to inspect the weather only to see a swarm of dancing midges in the still morning air, all eagerly awaiting to make a meal of you. You retreat back into the tent to consider the options. Do you:

Ⓐ Dive out of the tent regardless; dress, dismantle the tent at speed and make a quick getaway.

Ⓑ Perform a delicate contortionist's act to get packed and dressed within the tent, cover every bare patch of skin with insect repellent, and then proceed as above.

Ⓒ Jump out of the tent and hastily re-light the fire to try and smoke out the midges, thereby buying yourselves time for a more leisurely departure.

Ⓓ Stay in the tent playing cards for the remainder of the morning. Hopefully, the wind might pick up and blow the midges away, or the sun might break through and send the 'wee beasties' back to the ground.

Ⓔ Don't go camping on the west coast during midge season (between May and September) in the first place.

Comments

Never underestimate a cloud of hungry midges. If you try for the quick getaway, you will be virtually eaten alive before you can get the tent pegs out. Covering up and smearing on insect repellent will hold them off only for a while, but not enough to make a clean getaway. Smoke from a fire is of little use unless you are standing directly in its path, risking suffocation.

Waiting for the midges to clear is probably the best option if you have the time. They are at their worst in the mornings and evenings when the light is low and there is little or no breeze. Most canny Scots choose to go camping in the Highlands during early spring or autumn, when colder nights are more than compensated for by the absence of these infuriating wee beasties.

SITUATION 3

You're in a taxi chatting away to the driver when he completely flummoxes you by asking "Where do you stay?" Do you:

- **A** Tell him what country you're from.
- **B** Tell him where you happen to be staying that night.
- **C** Give him your home address and postcode.
- **D** Tell him the area, town, or city where you are living just now.
- **E** Explain again exactly where you want to be dropped off.

Comments

This common question throws most newcomers in Scotland, including visitors from England, Ireland and Wales. It means, where are you living at the moment? So the correct answer is **C**.

SITUATION 4

It's Friday night and you have just arrived in a bar with work colleagues for a few drinks. Everyone is in high spirits and eager to make a big night of it. You are happy to stay out with them but don't feel like drinking alcohol. You gingerly approach the bar to be confronted with an array of beers and spirits, as well as a fierce-looking barman waiting for your order. Do you:

- **A** Ask for a half of lemon shandy and explain to your friends and the barman alike that you are feeling a bit peaky.
- **B** Order a coffee and croissant and light up an imported Gittan cigarette with a continental air.
- **C** Ask for 'a pint of 80', throw open your wallet and ask what every one else is having. (A 'pint of 80' is a bitter brewed by MacEwans called 80 shillings. You will find it in most bars and if you're unsure as to what to have, it's a pretty good bet.)

Comments

Answer **C** is what will be expected of you. Pub culture, particularly on weekends, is all about buying rounds of drinks with your mates and generally getting blind drunk with them. Whoever should happen to arrive at the bar first is expected to buy everyone else a drink as well to start the ball rolling.

Women are no exception from the general peer pressure to drink heavily whilst on a big night out. In fact, in the spirit of equality between the sexes, women are expected to put down as much booze as the men and, if need be, carry them home at the end of it.

Ordering non-alcoholic shandy on arrival at a bar kind of defeats the object of the whole experience. It will also earn you mild derision from your work colleagues. If you go for the shandy regardless, be ready with a good excuse for your abstinence. Saying you feel unwell isn't enough; you'll end up being plied with that cure-all for every ailment: whisky. The best excuse is to say you have to drive home, even if you only live a stone's throw away from the bar.

Trying to rise above a boozing bar atmosphere by ordering coffee and patisseries is futile. You may as well not go in the first place.

SITUATION 5

You have just sat down for a dinner in the house of some new acquaintances, a retired and well-to-do couple called Alasdair and Fiona. This is the first time they have invited you over for a meal and you are keen to make a good impression. Everything is going well until the first course arrives, an inviting bowl of chicken and vegetable soup. It's been a long evening and you are hungry, so after politely waiting for the other guests to serve themselves, you smile broadly and tuck in. Moments later, Alasdair clears his throat and says, "Let us say grace and thank the Lord for the food we are about to receive." With your soup spoon already firmly lodged in your mouth, you will have to act fast to deliver yourself from the disapproval of your God-fearing guests. Do you:

Ⓐ Say three Hail Mary's and flagellate yourself with whatever comes to hand as penance, hoping that this will bring quick forgiveness before your soup goes cold.

ⓑ Wolf down the rest of the soup in time for the last Amen and the second course.

ⓒ Mumble an apology, gingerly lick the spoon clean and lay it back down until Alasdair has finished saying grace.

Comments

Self-flagellation is never a good idea, even in the most desperate of situations. If you continue eating through grace, you will be lucky if you even see the second course. The third option is the best one; your pious hosts will take note but won't pass comment until after you have left.

SITUATION 6

It's Friday night and you have been invited out for a big night on the town. You are to meet in a bar 30 minutes' walk away before moving on to a hot night of clubbing. It's blowing a howling gale outside and the condensation is freezing up on the windows. Taxi or no taxi, it's hellish cold out there. Swinging open the wardrobe door, you are faced with an array of choices. Do you plum for:

ⓐ Thermal underwear, heavy jumpers, two scarves and a wool-lined, tent-shaped long coat.

ⓑ A skimpy outfit for club land, natty jacket, and dark glasses.

ⓒ Settle for a quiet night by the fire with a mug of cocoa and wait on the spring to venture outside.

Comments

The sensible option is to stay in, although hibernation will do your social life no good. Bundling up in an ill-fitting combination of winter warmers is hardly urban cool, but it will stave off hypothermia. The best option is the most impractical—dress to impress and let the weather take care of itself. Ignoring the cold is the best way to overcome it and if everyone else flounces around in their glad rags in the heart of winter, why shouldn't you? Remember that a true Northerner is too hard to notice the cold and that whisky was invented in Scotland to keep you warm as much as to lighten the spirits.

SITUATION 7

You have been invited to your first *ceilidh*. You desperately want to go but haven't got a clue what to wear and have never danced a Scottish reel in your life. You don't know what the difference is between an eightsome reel and the Charlton, let alone how to negotiate dances like the Duke of Perth and the Gay Gordon. Do you:

Ⓐ Dash out and buy a book on Scottish reels to practice with the Hoover in front of the mirror. Or find a friend who is in the know and ask them to take you through some of the steps as preparation.

Ⓑ Politely decline the invitation and stay at home with your two left feet firmly tucked up in a pair of bedroom slippers.

Ⓒ Throw caution to the wind, go out and hire the full Highland outfit and throw yourself into the melee with more enthusiasm than sense.

Comments

If you decline the invitation, you'll needlessly miss out on a great night out. All but the most formal of Scottish *ceilidhs* are fun and easygoing. The easier reels are quick to pick up and if you take a wrong turn, someone will show you the way. You can always sit out the harder dances and soak up the atmosphere instead of making a complete fool of yourself. Doing your homework beforehand may help, but there is no better way to learn than by just turning up and having a go.

However, if you are a novice and go wearing a kilt, you will be expected to know what you are doing. Most *ceilidhs* have informal dress codes. Jeans and a shirt or T-shirt is fine for boys. Girls often choose to wear summer-style dresses to swirl around in although this is not expected. Of course, the Highland balls are considerably more formal affairs.

SITUATION 8

You have been invited for a few days' salmon fishing on the River Tay. Your experience of fishing is stumping around grimy rivers with a can of maggots and a hook and line as a child. You wander into a fish and tackle shop to buy a rod with no idea of what to come away with. Do you opt for:

A A short spinning rod with a combination of bright lures and Day-Glo imitation fish with barbed hooks protruding from their ends (called pugs).

B Settle for what you know and go for the budget option, some line, weights and a tub seething with maggots or worms.

C Splash out and buy an expensive carbon fibre fly rod with an assortment of feathered flies.

Comments

There is only one correct option for the salmon fisherman or woman in Scotland, the fly rod. You may have no idea of how to wield it and virtually no chance of landing anything larger than stray leaves but that isn't the point. The whole exercise is as much an art as a sport and there is nothing more satisfying than beating the odds to land your first proper fish. There will also be a local gamekeeper, called a *ghillie*, on hand to show you the ropes. Salmon fishing with a spinner may bring quicker results, but it is considered unsporting and is frowned upon. If you appear with worms or maggots, you may be mistaken for a poacher and have to beat a hasty retreat from an irate *ghillie*.

DO'S AND DON'TS

DO'S

- Do be hospitable in your own home. If someone comes to your place, immediately offer them something to drink, be it an electrician fixing the oven or a lifelong friend.

- Be polite and chatty at all times. The Scots are a friendly bunch and like to be acknowledged, so do say hello and ask people how they are regardless of whether they are a friend, someone in a shop or, in more rural areas, just a passerby.

- Do hold eye contact when you shake someone's hand and don't kiss them on the cheek unless you know them well.

- Do watch your language and always be respectful with the elderly. If you are in one of the areas in the Highlands where the Free Church has sway, do strictly observe the Sabbath. This means no work whatsoever on a Sunday— even going for a walk or putting out the washing is frowned upon.

- Do give way to local boy racers and belligerent farmers on single-track roads—they take few prisoners.

- Do give money to the homeless, it's cold out there and they need as much help as they can get.

- If you owe someone money, do remember to repay them, they may not remind you but they are unlikely to forget.

- If a formal invitation for a dinner or wedding calls for black tie, do go in a tuxedo and a bow tie rather than a dark suit with a black tie.

- Do say sorry if you bump into someone, not to mention if they bump into you.

- If you are fly fishing, do always wear a hat. This isn't as much a question of etiquette as a necessity to avoid ending up with an unwanted ear piercing from an errant cast.

- Do try chips with salt and sauce, *haggis* and battered Mars bars, they are all much tastier than they sound!

- Do read *Oor Wullie*, the cartoon adventures of the mischievous wee Glasgow lad in *The Sunday Post*. This much loved cartoon has been running for years and is a great introduction to Scottish humour and the Glasgow patter.

DON'TS

- Don't refuse an offer of a drink in someone else's home, unless you are a good friend or just passing through. This is especially true in the Highlands of Scotland where it is polite to accept the waist-stretching array of biscuits and cake that is often passed to guests. If you are invited to dinner, remember, if possible, to return the invitation within a few weeks.

- Don't catch eyes with groups of young men, particularly if you are a young man yourself. Eye contact, especially on a Friday or Saturday night on the town, can be misinterpreted as a challenge for a fight.

- Don't be afraid to voice your opinions. Apart from formal occasions, you can generally be honest about how you feel about things, especially politics. However, don't open up too quickly about your private life; it takes time to gain true confidence, and tongues may wag in smaller communities.

- Don't interrupt an exchange of pleasantries mid-flow, even if you are in a hurry. There is never too little time for a chat in Scotland.

- Don't photograph people without first asking their permission.

- Don't be offended if you hear swear words, especially in Glasgow where they are often part of the daily patter.

- Don't go and drink in a bar on your own if you are a woman. If you are with a female friend, that's fine. Men can, and do, drink alone. If someone includes you in a round of drinks, don't order a hugely expensive drink, like a fancy cocktail, unless you are willing to buy the same for every one else when your turn comes round. If someone calls a toast, remember to raise your glass. If someone lightly makes fun of you, laugh rather than take offence; it's all in good humour.

- Don't ask strangers for cigarettes, they are far too expensive in Britain to be given away freely.

- If you wear a kilt, don't wear a tartan that you aren't entitled to wear (your parents or grandparents should have the appropriate clan name). Never reveal what you are wearing underneath a kilt, especially if it's nothing.

- Don't claim to be Scottish just because one of your grand-parents was.
- Don't make disparaging remarks about Scotland or its people. Scots are fiercely proud of their nation and while they have no problem laughing at themselves, they don't take criticism lightly from foreigners, especially the English.
- Never vocally support English international rugby or football, especially if they are playing Scotland. Supporting an English football league side is okay.
- Don't call whisky 'bourbon' or 'scotch'.

GLOSSARY

It is impossible to squeeze into one chapter what could be a lifetime's work. So the following can only be a taster of some of the most commonly used Scots words and expressions.

Introductions	
Alright there big man?	Hello there
Cheerio	Goodbye
Cheers pal	Can mean thank you or goodbye
Hiya	Hello
How're you doing?	How are you?
I'm no bad, and yerself?	I'm OK, how about you?
See you Jimmy/ Alright Jimmy	Name given to anyone, being as common as it is. Usually said ironically as it has become such a cliché
What have you(s) been up tae?	It is common to say 'yous' when talking to more than one person.
You alright pal?	Are you ok?

The Weather	
Haar	East coast sea mist that occasionally comes inland
It's a grand day	Usually grey but without rain
Missle/spitting/pishing it down/wet out/drookit	Differing ways of describing rain
The nights are fair drawing in	It's getting darker earlier
There's a wee nip in the air	It's cold

Food and Drink	
Bevvy	An alcoholic drink
Brekkie	Breakfast
Fish supper	Fish and chips
Juice	Describes all soft drinks
Last orders	'Last orders at the bar' is called just before closing time, giving patrons the chance to get in a last drink. 'Time' is shouted when it's time to leave
Long vodka	Scottish cocktail which mixes vodka, lime, tonic water and angostura bitters
Piece	Sandwich
Pished/guttered/smashed/reekin/fleain/absolutely steamin'	These terms are used to describe varying levels of intoxication
Pokey hat	99 flake ice cream
Scran	Food
Tea/supper	Dinner

The Land	
Ben	Hill
Black house	Thick-walled traditional house
Bothy	Shepherds mountain shelter
Brae	Slope, hill
Brig	Bridge
Burn	Stream
Cairn	Pile of stones at the peak of hills and mountains
Corrie	Smaller valley between hills
Croft	Small cottage and area of land

The Land	
Dolmen	Grave chamber
Dyke	Old stone division of land
Glen	Valley
Inch	Small island
Kirk	Church
Kyle	Narrow strait or channel
Lazy bed	Old crofting system of agriculture still maintained in areas such as the Outer Hebrides. The thin soil has poor drainage. To improve the soil's productivity, vegetable patches are raised and laid over with seaweed, manure and thatch for fertiliser. The channels between them provide drainage
Links	Land running next to the sea
Loch	Lake
Lochan	Small lake
Manse	Official house of a presbyterian minister
Moor	Open plain
Strath	Broad, flat river valley
Runrig	A system by which rural communities would rotate their corps, sharing out the land and it's resources and ensuring that no one area was over cultivated. Runrig is also the name of a monumental eighties Scottish rock band

Gaelic Place Names

The individual names of places in Gaelic don't just sound good to the ear. They offer up wisdom on the significance that earlier people gave to their local area. Translate local place names and an unseen world opens up; where language, place, history and identity becomes bonded in light and stone. Take some of the names around the central highland town of Pitlochry as an example. The following is a translation of some of the local land marks.

Ben-y-Vrackie	The speckled mountain named after the white flashes of quarts on the mountain, now long since quarried
Craigower	The goats tower
Faskally	The resting place in the wood
Fonab	Abbots' land
Loch Tummel	Lake of the hot stream
Killiecrankie	Wood of the aspen tree
Moulin	Smooth, rounded hill
Pitlochry	Comes from a mix of Pictish and Gaelic. It means 'The place of the sentinel stone' (*pit-cloich-aire*). it is speculated that the town marks an old guarding place for the Picts against the Romans
Port-na-Craig	Ferry by the rock. The rock is still in the river Tummel, although the ferry has long since has long since been replaced by a suspension bridge

Words and Phrases	
A good crack/a real hoot	A good time

Words and Phrases

Aye	'Aye' means yes and much more. It can be used as a short and crisp affirmative or a drawn out to give agreement to a point of discussion. It can simply be said to gently fill a silence. Old boys in bars punctuate lulls in conversation with the occasional 'aye'
Bairn	Baby
Barry	Good (Edinburgh term)
Blether	To talk
Boggin	Revolting
Bonnie	Beautiful
Go for a burn	To go for a fast drive or cycle
By the way	Used all the time as punctuation in speech
Chancer	Someone who is sly or opportunistic
Chum	To keep company with: 'Chum tae the shop'
Curls your teeth	Tastes horrible
Dinnae hav the willies	Don't get scared
Do you ken?	Do you understand/know?
Dram	Measure of whisky
Dreich	Wet and miserable weather
Earn you keep	Pay your way
Face like a bust couch	An ugly person
Face like a bulldog licking piss off a thistle	Another ugly person
Feart	Fear
Fine fettle	In good form
Fluke	Lucky break

Words and Phrases	
Folk	People
Fucking cracked it!	To finish or overcome something
Gagy	Boy or man
Greet	To cry ('Stop yur greeting')
Galore	Gaelic word meaning 'enough'
Gimme two secs	I'll be with you in a second
Glasgow kiss	Head butt
Heebie jeebies	Scared
Hen	Woman
Hummin	Smells really bad
I don't have a scoobie	I have no idea
I've got the glass on you	I've been watching you (a Highland phrase)
Jakey	Alcoholic or junkie
Jiggered	Exhausted
Jock	Mildly derogatory term for a Scot. However the Scots call each other jock
Lass	Woman
Mac	Son of
Mackle	Big
Mental	Crazy. It's common to say 'totally mental'
Mingin	Disgusting
Muckle /peedie	Small. Peedie is an Orkney word
Nay bother	Don't worry/no problem
Nips your head/a wee bit nippy	Something that is frustrating
Off the sauce	Not drinking alcohol
Old reekie	Edinburgh

Words and Phrases	
Pal	Friend
Radge	Foul
Sair	Sore
Sassenach	Southerner
Shuftie	To have a quick look at something
Skeemie	Someone who lives in one of the poor housing estates or 'schemes'
Skelp	To smack or hit
Sketchy	Dubious
Sleakit	Someone who is sly
Snooty	Pretentious
Soon faced	Glum
Spare prick at a wedding	Standing out, not fitting in
Spawney	Lucky
Stour	Dust
Swithering	Wracked with indecision
That's champion	That's brilliant
The pictures	The movies
The wiege	Glasgow
To have the glad eye	To fancy someone
Toonie	Someone from a town or city
Wee	Small
What er ye like	What are you like
Whitie	Moment of total panic
Wing it	To get through a difficult situation by chance alone
Workies	Builders
Yen	Man
Yer ma	I don't believe you

Words and Phrases	
You beauty/oh ya fucking beautie	Fantastic
You must be joking	You can't be serious

RESOURCE GUIDE

The following list of Internet sites should quench the most insatiable of thirsts for information on Scotland. I have chosen more established sites that are regularly updated and unlikely to disappear overnight into the virtual ether.

EMERGENCIES AND HEALTH

- National Health System (NHS)
  Website: http://www.nhs.uk
  400 pages of information, history and advice from the heart of Britain's welfare state.
- Disabled Information
  Website: http://www.disabledinfo.com
  A comprehensive database of information for disabled people, with good links to other relevant sites.

HOME AND FAMILY

- Prime Location
  Website: http://www.primelocation.com
  A good place to start if you are renting or buying.

- Scottish Solicitors Property Centres
  Website: http://www.sspc.co.uk
  Information of properties to rent or buy from solicitors is pooled on this site. From the homepage page, you can click through to see properties in any part of Scotland.
- Scottish Tourist Board Official Website
  Website: http://www.visitscotland.com
  This Scottish Tourist Board site gives a good list of places to stay while you are exploring Scotland.
- Youth Hostels Association
  Website: http://www.yha.org.uk
  One of the best budget options for touring Scotland on a shoestring.
- Universities and Colleges Admissions Service for the UK (UCAS)
  Website: http://www.ucas.ac.uk
  Everything you need to know about choosing and getting into higher education.
- The Inland Revenue
  Website: http://www.inlandrevenue.gov.uk
  The official source on all your tax needs, you can even fill in your tax forms here online.

ENTERTAINMENT AND LEISURE

- Scotland's Internet Directory
  Website: http://www.scotlandinter.net
  Boasts over 7,000 links to theatre, music, cinema, and much more!
- Edinburgh Festivals
  Website: http:// www.edinburghfestivals.co.uk
  A good source of festival information for the city's summer madness.
- Ebay
  Website: http://www.ebay.co.uk
  The shopping craze for second hand goods that has taken the world by storm.
- Find any Film
  Website: http://findanyfilm.com

Type in the cinema locations closest to you and find out what is showing at the local cinemas.

- Scottish Theatre Web
  Website: nationaltheatresscotland.com
  Keep abreast of what's going on in the world of theatre with this fun, informal site.
- Scottish Book Trust
  Website: http:// www.scottishbooktrust.com
  Latest events, gossip and reviews from the Scottish book industry.
- Amazon
  Website: http://www.amazon.co.uk
  Order books, CDs, DVDs, or even household appliances and outdoor furniture online.

TRANSPORT AND COMMUNICATIONS

- UK Travel
  Website: http://www.lonelyplanet.com/scotland
  Good general information on everything from visas, car hire and ferries to good eateries and places to stay along the way.
- Cheap Flights
  Website: http://www.cheapflights.co.uk
  This website pools cheap deals and offers and is a good place to shop around for bargains.
- Ryan Air
  Website: http://www.ryanair.com
  On-line booking site for cheap flights in and around the UK.
- Easy Jet
  Website: http://www.easyjet.com
  Cheap flights around Europe, including Edinburgh to London.
- Rail Travel Information
  Website: http://www.nationalrail.co.uk/
  Up-to-date train information.
- Eurostar
  Website: http://www.eurostar.com

For express travel by train from London to Paris, you can book on-line at Eurostar's website.

- Ferrybooker
  Website: http://www.ferrybooker.com
  The most comprehensive of online booking sites for passage by sea to or from the British Isles.
- Caledonian MacBrayne
  Website: http://www.calmac.co.uk
  This is the site for most ferry crossings to the small isles in Scotland. You can book your tickets from here in advance. The website also has links to tour operators offering holiday packages.
- National Express
  Website: http:// www.nationalexpress.com
  For travel by coach between principal cities in Scotland and the UK.
- Driver and Vehicle Licensing Agency
  Website: http://www.dvla.gov.uk/
  For all information on driving licences, including how to get an international driving permit from abroad.
- The Automobile Association (AA)
  Website: http://www.theaa.com/
  A comprehensive site for drivers, including maps, travel information, hotel guide and quick insurance quotes.
- Royal Automobile Association (RAC)
  Website: http://www.rac.co.uk
  More good information and advice for motorists.
- Map 24
  Website: http:// www.uk.map24.com
  Find the exact location of any address in the country, or map out your own route through Scotland on this user-friendly website.

MEDIA

- BBC News
  Website: http://news.bbc.co.uk
  Catch the breaking stories on this pioneering site by the British Broadcasting Corporation, better known as the BBC or the 'beeb'.

- Scottish Media Links
  Website: http://www.wikipedia.org/wiki/media_in_scotland
  The Gateway to Scotland site has this link page to all the major Scottish newspapers as well as Scottish television.

LANGUAGE

- The British Council in Scotland
  Website: http://www.britishcouncil.org
  The cream, and also the most expensive, of the English language schools in Scotland.

RELIGION

- The Church of Scotland
  Website: http://www.churchofscotland.org.uk/
- The Free Church of Scotland
  Website: http://www.freechurch.org
- The Catholic Church
  Website: http://www.catholic-church.org.uk
- The Hindu Universe
  Website: http://www.hindunet.org
- The Islamic Digest
  Website: http://www.islamicdigest.net
- The Muslim News
  Website: http://www.muslimnews.co.uk

GENERAL COUNTRY INFORMATION

- Rampant Scotland Directory
  Website: http://www.rampantscotland.com
  A quick way to hunt for information on Scotland, however bizarre.
- British Politics Page
  Website: http://www.ukpol.co.uk
  A good starting point for learning about politics in Scotland and Great Britain. This site has over 15,000 links to other political web-pages.
- Scottish Government
  Website: http://www.scotland.gov.uk
  Read about the ins and outs of the Scottish parliament, and keep up-to-date with breaking stories.

- Home Office
  Website: http://www.homeoffice.gov.uk
  Useful government site complete with visa and immigration information and advice.
- The Department of Work and Pensions
  Website: http://www.dss.gov.uk/
  UK government agency offering benefits advice and general information on what is available for those who are financially challenged.
- Citizens Advice Bureaux (CAB)
  Website: http://www.citizensadvice.org.uk
  Free advice on anything from housing to immigration law. The Citizens Advice Bureaux has offices in most cities and towns.

BUSINESS INFORMATION

- Scottish Enterprise Network
  Website: http://www.scottish-enterprise.com
  Good information on business advice, news and networking opportunities in Scotland.
- UK Directory
  Website: http://www.ukdirectory.co.uk
  A comprehensive database of business related websites in the UK.
- The London Stock Exchange
  Website: http://www.londonstockexchange.com/
  Follow the ups and downs of the stock market from the comfort of your own PC.

FURTHER READING

JOURNEYS THROUGH TIME AND PLACE

A Journey to the Western Isles of Scotland and *The Journal of a Tour to the Hebrides*. Samuel Johnson and James Boswell. Edinburgh, Scotland: Canongate Books Ltd, 2001.
- The most famous account of a journey round the islands.

Scottish Journey. Edwin Muir. Edinburgh, Scotland: Mainstream Publishing, 1996.
- Another classic Scottish travelogue. Written in 1935, it covers much of Scotland before the Second World War. But it isn't dated; the landscapes, people and social commentary offer lasting echoes of Scotland today.

A Search for Scotland. R F Mackenzie. London, UK: Fontana Press, 1991.
- A very personal trip into Mackenzie's own cultural roots, touching on most aspects of Scots culture with a wry and sometimes critical eye. The book is currently out of print, but is easy to pick up in a library or second-hand bookshop.

On the Crofters' Trail. David Craig. London, UK: Pimlico, 2007.
- The best modern account of the Highland Clearances, told through interviews with descendants.

Jessie's Journey. Jess Smith. Edinburgh, Scotland: Mercat Press, 2003.
- An intimate account of the author Jess Smith's life travelling around Scotland as gipsy. The book had such success that she has since followed up with more accounts of now distant times, including *Tales from the Tent* (Edinburgh, Scotland: Mercat Press, 2003) and *Tears for a Tinker* (Edinburgh, Scotland: Mercat Press, 2005)

HISTORY AND POLITICS

Scotland: A New History. Michael Lynch. London, UK: Pimlico, 1992.

- The best all-round history book. Lynch manages the impossible; to compress a broad narrative of Scots history since the times of Picts into one volume. Lynch has since edited the *Oxford Companion to Scottish History* (UK: University Oxford, 2001), a superlative reference book with both hard facts and analysis in a dictionary format.

A History of Scotland, J D Mackie. London, UK: Penguin, 1991.

- Another good study that doesn't get too bogged down in details.

Scotland Road Trip. John Prebble. London, UK: Pimlico, 2000.

- Personal reflection on the country and it's troubled history. For more in-depth studies on certain aspects of Scottish history, John Prebble stands head and shoulders above the rest. He wrote captivating books on the massacre of Glencoe, Culloden, and the Highland clearances back in the 1960s and 1970s.

- Historic Scotland (Stationery Office/Seven Mills) publishes a whole range of cheerful guides on Scotland's history and prehistory, complete with stunning photographs. Their guide to Scotland's castles is particularly good.

When Scotland Ruled the World. Stewart Lamont. London, UK: HarperCollins, 2001.

- A bold account of Scotland's achievements in letters, science and exploration during the age of enlightenment.

Collins Clans and Tartans. London, UK: Collins, 2005.

- A good way to understand more about Scotland's old feudal society is to read up on clan history. This book gives a good, if brief, history.

Scottish Surnames and Families. Donald Whyte. Edinburgh, Scotland: Birlinn Publishers, 2000.

- An in-depth read about the history behind Scottish names.

Who Owns Scotland. Andy Wightman. Edinburgh, Scotland: Canongate, 2000.

- A contemporary outlook on Scotland's continued feudal system of land ownershiphas. This book has become a classic reference book for those calling for reform.

MYTH AND LEGEND

Scottish Fairy and Folk Tales. Ed. Sir George Douglas. Mineola, NY: Dover Publications, 2000.

- A reprint of a centuries old classic. The Scots can be difficult to digest in places but the stories themselves are captivating.

The Folklore of the Scottish Highlands. Anne Ross. Gloucestershire, UK: Tempus, 2000.

- For a more modern and slightly more academic approach to clan lore, witchcraft and other superstitions.

Myths and Legends of the Celts. James Mackillop. London, UK: Penguin, 2005.

- Gives an equally rigorous account with lots of background history thrown in.

LANGUAGE

The Concise Scots Dictionary. Edinburgh, Scotland: Polygon, 2003.

- For more extensive coverage.

The Complete Patter. Michael Munro. Edinburgh, Scotland: Birlinn, 2007.

- Glasgow has a particularly fast and entertaining dialect and this book does it justice.

Scottish Gaelic in Three Months. Robert O'Mullally, John MacInnes. London, UK: Dorling Kindersley, 1998.
- Covers basic pronunciation, vocabulary and grammar in step-by-step lessons.

Gaelic Dictionary. Malcolm MacLennan. Edinburgh, Scotland: Mercat Press, 1992; Ottawa, Canada: Laurier Books Ltd, 2005.
- A good reference work.

Scotland's Place Names. David Dorward. Edinburgh, Scotland: Mercat Press, 1998.
- Makes easy sense of many of the Gaelic place names without turning them into an endless list.

GUIDES

Scotland the Best: The One True Guide. Peter Irvine. London, UK: HarperCollins, 2006.
- As popular with residents of Scotland as it is with visitors. Bookstores in Scotland are littered with guides. The ubiquitous *Lonely Planet* and *Rough Guide* series are the best known for all-round travel information. Both are pretty comprehensive and regularly updated.

Reading Glasgow. Moira Burgess. Edinburgh, Scotland: Scottish Book Trust, 1998.

The Literary Companion to Edinburgh. Andrew Lowne. London, UK: Methuen Publishing, 2001.
- Good bets for a quirkier look at Scotland's principle cities.

OUTDOOR PURSUITS

The Munros—Scotland's Highest Mountains. Cameron McNeish. Edinburgh, Scotland: Lomond Books, 2009.
- A good coffee table book for climbing Scotland's Munros. Filled with detail, maps and photographs of the 248 mountains over 3000 meters in Scotland, some of the proceeds from sales are also donated to the Mountain Rescue Service.

The Munro Almanac. Cameron McNeish. Northampton, MA: Interlink Publishing, 2000.

- A good pocket companion. His latest book, *An Encyclopedia of Places and Landscape* (UK: Collins, 2006), is the definitive reference guide to the country.

Ordnance Survey Pathfinder Guides. Norwich, UK: Jarrold Publishing, 1999.

- Have clearly laid out maps with colour coded routs. Ordinance Survey also produces the most detailed maps of the whole of the British Isles designed for orienteering with a compass.

The West Highland Way. Bob Aitken and Roger Smith. Edinburgh, Scotland: Mercat Press, 2006.

- Includes local history and photos along the way.

The Best Courses in Scotland by Golf World. London, UK: Aurum Press, 2000.

- Provides contact details, ratings and reviews on golf courses in Scotland.

AA Guide to Golf Courses UK. UK: AA Publishing, 2008.

- A comprehensive companion which includes listings of places to stay.

FOOD AND DRINK

The New Scottish Cookery Book. Nick Nairn. London, UK: BBC Book Pub, 2004.

- Nick Nairn has joined the ranks of celebrity chef stardom in recent years. This book gives a sumptuous new take on traditional Scottish cooking.

Scottish Kitchen. Sue Lawrence. London, UK: Headline Books, 2003.

- Gives quick immersion into Scots cuisine with both traditional and modern recipes, together with mouthwatering photos.

Scottish Cooking. Catherine Brown. Trowbridge, UK: Redwood Books, 1999.
- An extensive handbook. Covers everything from home baking to the lifestyles and cooking times of wild game.

The Whisky Trails. Gordon Brown. UK: Prion Books, 2000.
- Gives a comprehensive and up-to-date guide to the distilleries trail, including information on other nearby sites of local interest.

Malt Whisky Companion. Michael Jackson. London, UK: Dorling Kindersley, 2004.
- A more definitive guide on all aspects of whisky

PICTURE BOOKS

Colin Baxter's monopoly on landscape photography in Scotland has slipped in recent years. He is now joined by a number of published landscape photographers, including Colin Prior, Craig McMaster and Sampson Lloyd.

Scotland's Century: 1900–2000. Edinburgh, Scotland: Lomond Books, 2000.
- For the people side of Scotland and full of striking images.

Shades of Scotland 1959–1988. Oscar Marzaroli. Text by James Grassie. Edinburgh, Scotland: Maintream Publishing, 1989.
- Another classy mix of portraits and landscape.

The Hebredians. Gus Wylie. Edinburgh, Scotland: Birlinn, 2005.
- A book of black and white photos of the people of the small isles that spans 30 years.

Rebus's Scotland, A Personal Journey. Ian Rankin. London, UK: Orion Books, 2005.
- Visits the places through photographs and words that have inspired him to write crime fiction set in Edinburgh.

GENERAL

The Encyclopaedia of Scotland. Ed. Julia Keay and John Keay. London, UK: Collins, 2000.
- An awesome reference book on everything you wanted to know about Scotland but were afraid to ask.

Whitaker's Almanack 2009. London, UK: A&C Black Publishing, 2009.
- Packed with information and useful addresses.

ABOUT THE AUTHOR

Jamie Grant spent many years as a boy living in a small village on the west coast of Scotland. Here he learnt the subtle arts of stone-throwing and jellyfish-stamping long before he heard of the likes of Flora Macdonald or the colourists.

His total immersion in all things Scottish came later in life. After going to university in Cardiff, he spent the best part of his twenties in South America, working as an English teacher, journalist and photographer. Whilst nearly drowning in an Amazon river, he had a vision of his distant homeland and decided to make the long pilgrimage back to Scotland. On return, he found everything he had dreamt of and nothing he had expected. Jamie lives in Scotland with his wife Fiona and son Tom.

INDEX